WRIGHTS LANE

*To my new friend
Wendy
... welcome to my
world!*

Dick Wright

WRIGHTS LANE

COME ON IN

DICK WRIGHT

Copyright © 2009 by DICK WRIGHT.

ISBN: Hardcover   978-1-4415-5203-7
             Softcover   978-1-4415-5202-0

All rights reserved. No part of this book may be reproduced or transmitted in any form or by any means, electronic or mechanical, including photocopying, recording, or by any information storage and retrieval system, without permission in writing from the copyright owner.

This book was printed in the United States of America.

To order additional copies of this book, contact:
Xlibris Corporation
1-888-795-4274
www.Xlibris.com
Orders@Xlibris.com
63715

CONTENTS

DEDICATION

Wrights Lane is dedicated to everyone who choses to *"Come on In"* and without whom my effort would be wasted.

INTRODUCTION

"WRIGHTS LANE" IS a collection of memories and personal reflections on life, most of which have appeared in newspaper columns and on my web site of the same name. I have been motivated in this project by a number of friends and relatives who have suggested bringing some of my humble ramblings together in book form. So this is something tangible that you can hold in your hand, pick up at your leisure, and share with others.

You will not discover anything overly profound on these pages. I do hope, however, that readers will find meaningful hidden messages and fodder for thought in my collective experiences and musings. I like to think of my work as conversational. You may agree or disagree. You may smile. You may shed a tear. There is also the outside chance that there will be something motivational in some of my thoughts and extracts and if so, the objective of this book has been realized.

Incidentally, Wrights Lane is the name of a real street in my home town of Dresden, Ontario, and it is no coincidence that the actual street sign appears on the cover. Ideally, Wrights Lane will be a comfortable place to visit.

So come on in . . . Stay a while . . . Kick off your shoes if you want to. Pour yourself a cup of coffee. If you follow my lead, a nice relaxing glass of wine may be in order. In fact, you may want to come back for several more visits like this one because there is a lot to talk about.

Its so nice to have you!

—Dick

CHAPTER 1

A DREAM DATE

"A DREAM DATE" is really a story for readers of all ages. For those in my age group, I suggest allowing your mind to drift back a half century to the early 1950s. For those fortunate enough to be younger, this can be an imaginative journey to an era when life was considerably more simple and innocent than at present.

Picture nickle-a-play juke boxes, 10-cent double dip ice cream cones, 10-cent cherry cokes, 25-cent movies, 15-cent loaves of bread, 25-cent quarts of milk delivered to your door, Toni home permanents, crinolines, bobby sox and saddle shoes, fall fairs and teen dances. Imagine too, before-television evenings spent with ears glued to the radio listening to Jack Benny, Amos N' Andy, Duffy's Tavern, Lux Radio Theatre and Bing Crosby, Perry Como, Rosemary Clooney or Dinah Shore. Then there was the institution known as Foster Hewitt and his hockey broadcasts from the gondola at Maple Leafs Gardens, his distinctive voice calling: "Hello Canada and hockey fans coast to coast . . . welcome to Hockey Night in Canada!"

This is a story cast in a period when young people were seen but not necessarily always heard, when elders were respected, when friendship was nurtured, when carefree time was available for simple day dreaming and fantasizing about the future.

A grandfatherly Louis St. Laurent was Canadian prime minister of the day and Leslie Frost was Premier of the Province of Ontario.

The setting could well be any small town in Southwestern Ontario in the 1950s. There is also a good chance that the lead character(s) in the story could be someone like you—or I. Then again maybe someone you know comes to mind. Regardless, it is my hope that "A Dream Date" may provide a form of encouragement for some young person who is struggling with shyness and a lack of self-confidence, something that we all experienced to varying degrees in our formative years.

Oh, I almost forgot . . . This is a true story. Only the names have been changed to protect the innocent.

He did not know which was worse, his throbbing head, his upset stomach, or the ache in his heart. Young Nick White was not actually sick, at least not in a physical sense. His problem was more of a case of tug-of-waritis, an infliction that often strikes 17-year-old males when awakening hormones pull in one direction and youthful inhibitions tug in another.

Nick could not escape his malady, not even in the solitude of his bedroom. Through an open window came waves of lively music, punctuated by youthful laughter and shrieks of excitement from the town's only high school, less than an eighth of a mile away. Colorful print curtains fluttered softly against Nick's furrowed brow, as if caressed by the gentle June evening breeze.

Sprawled across his bed and using the window ledge to support his elbows as he cradled his chin in his hands, Nick stared into the darkness of night. Sad eyes transfixed the large, brightly illuminated school auditorium windows little more than a stone's throw beyond his back yard. Ever so faintly he could see tips of red and white streamers on the wall inside and a portion of a huge banner.

"Welcome to Prom Night 1955." Welcome? . . . Everyone but Nick White! The highlight event of the school year and he was not there to enjoy it because of his hesitation in asking a certain young lady to accompany him. "I'd probably be refused anyway," Nick rationalized with increasing self pity.

He grimaced, recalling how he had ruined any potential for a date with his Number One choice. Susan was an honor student, a cheerleader and had the prettiest, long auburn hair that Nick had ever seen. So enamored and distracted was he when passing her in chemistry class one day that he tripped over his own two feet and sprawled headlong into an experiment she had just completed. He could still hear the laughter that erupted in the lab that devastating day. He shivered with the vision of Miss Gibson, the teacher, who could only shake her head in disbelief as she attempted to conceal a smile by feigning a cough.

Sheepishly picking up shattered beaker and test tube glass and trying to avoid eye contact with Susan, he'd thought: " . . . guess I won't be asking her to the prom any time soon." Hours of fantasizing—his arms around Susan on the dance floor and admiring glances of his friends—all dashed in one clumsy, awkward moment.

Tears welled in his eyes and his chin quivered as he reminded himself of the three other substitute prom date prospects he dared telephone in the previous 72 hours, only to hang up each time before someone answered. "What a dummy!"

Nick wanted desperately to be outgoing and spontaneous but there was always something holding him back. Personality disorders of this nature were particularly problematic for a young man in a post World War Two society that was beginning to encourage, and reward, spontaneity in its youth. His shyness was beginning to be mistaken for arrogance and he was often accused of being "stuck up". Teachers, in fact, had given up on attempts to "draw him out" and he was dismissed as an under-achiever whose only interest was in playing sports.

The self doubt, the frustration, the helplessness. It was all too much for his post pubescent mind. Suppressed emotions erupted. He collapsed, face down, into the downy softness of the pillow that, all too often in recent months, had become his refuse and comforter. His lean body convulsed spasmodically as he wept with muffled gasps that came from deep within his heaving chest.

In a matter of minutes the pillow was drenched from tears that cascaded down his flushed cheeks. Exhausted and emotionally spent, Nick turned his back to the window and the troubling distractions that it framed. Blinking rapidly, he attempted to clear the watery blur from his eyes.

In the haze of semi darkness he could see the magazine photographs of baseball heroes he had painstakingly thumb tacked to the plywood walls of his bedroom—Ted Williams, Joe DiMaggio, Bob Feller, Jackie Robinson, Yogi Berra. He imagined a photo of himself, smiling proudly in New York Yankees pinstripes, surrounded by his pinup heroes.

"Some day!" he thought to himself. The imaginative distraction took only a few minutes to work its wonder and Nick drifted off to sleep. A sweet, welcome escape.

A LESSON IN STEPPING OUTSIDE OF YOURSELF

"WHAT'S THE MATTER, son? Is something troubling you?" Nick immediately recognized the deep, kindly voice coming from the outline of a figure standing over him.

"Oh, its you Dad! How did you know.?"

"I just had a feeling you were struggling with something," replied his father.

"Well the truth is, I really wanted to go to the high school prom tonight but I couldn't get a date," Nick answered, hoping to avoid further embarrassment.

"You couldn't get a date? A good looking star athlete like you?"

"Very funny Dad, but there's a little more to it than that. I couldn't get a date because I was too afraid to ask a girl and right now I really hate myself. What's wrong with me anyway?"

"Okay! Now I'm beginning to understand," said his father as he glanced knowingly out the window. "Let's just back up a bit and take this slowly, one step at a time." Nick had always submitted to his father's lectures with trepidation, but on this occasion every fibre in his body cried out for help.

"You remind me of myself when I was your age," his father continued. "Like you, I didn't have brothers or sisters and I grew up in a rather insular, self-centred world. I was not naturally outgoing and I, too, shied away from most social interaction. In time, however, I learned that in order to function effectively in the world and to gain what I wanted out of life, I had to force myself to step out of my comfort zone from time to time."

He explained that at one stage in his life it seemed that he was enclosed in a glass bubble. He could see out and yet he could not accept what he saw. As a result, he withdrew further into the bubble and now he was detecting the same troubling warning signs in his son.

"I want you to learn from my experience, Nick, because life is so mysterious and wonderful, it would be a shame if you should miss out on so much of it because of a lack of confidence in yourself, or a lack of faith in others," he added, pausing to make sure his words were sinking in.

"If I had one wish for you, it would be that you could learn by some means other than experience. But experience is the best teacher and what you are going through now will make you a better person in the long run, providing you handle it properly.

Do you understand what I'm trying to say to you, Nicky?"

"Yes, I think I do, Dad. But . . ."

Nick stopped in mid sentence as a strong arm gripped him around the shoulders. Drawn into his father's heavy cabinet maker's chest, he could smell a familiar tobacco and wood musk and a warm tingling sensation rushed through his stiff upper torso.

"We're going to try a little exercise," said his father without waiting for an answer to his question and gently nudging the two of them toward a telephone that sat on a highly polished, ornate table in the hall just a few steps from Nick's bedroom.

"When we get to the phone, I want you to pull away from me. In your mind's eye, envision stepping outside of your body, leaving your shyness and lack of confidence behind. Then pick up the receiver and dial Susan Turner's home number, but this time let the phone ring until someone answers and . . . well, you'll just naturally know what to do after that. OK, son?"

"But, wait a minute Dad. Why did you pick Susan Turner?" asked a very puzzled Nick.

"Because she's a nice girl and you like her, dummy," was his smiling father's curt reply.

"Seriously, you know how to focus when you're up to bat with runners in scoring position?" he added, picking up on his role as a baseball coach. "Well, in this case, focus on what you want to say to Susan and then say it with conviction. Aniticipate a positive response, because I have a sneeking suspicion that your feelings for her are mutual.

"You will find that it gets easier to express yourself and to reach out to others every time you use this 'stepping outside of yourself' technique. It won't be long before you are doing it without even thinking. Now, are you ready?"

"Okay. What ever you say, Dad, but I sure hope you're right about Susan. Here goes!"

A BREAKTHROUGH CALL
WITH GLORIOUS RESULTS

"NICK, FOR HEAVEN'S sake, wake up!" The sheet that was partially covering his still fully clad body was suddenly and unceremoniously stripped away. "Good Lord boy, you must have been tired last night. You didn't even take the time to undress."

"What . . . Is that you, Mom?" Nick groaned, squinting through sleep-swollen eyes.

"Yes, of course it's me. Come on, get up! We've got a lot of things to do today and I also want you to go to the cemetery with me this afternoon. Your Dad died three years ago today. Remember?"

"Oh, right. It doesn't seem that long ago, does it?" he answered, giving his mother a token hug as he struggled unsteadily to his feet.

Nick's father was only 48 years of age when he died of a sudden heart attack, leaving his devestated young wife with a void and limited resources to maintain a household and raise a teenage son. Mother and son formed a partnership that helped get them over the rough spots and they were managing reasonably well.

"Time passes quickly, Nicky," agreed his mother. With a glistening tear leaving its trail on one delicate cheek, she struggled to retain composure. "You lost your dad at a time when a boy needs a father most . . . It's just not fair."

"Ya, but I sometimes dream about him," Nick interjected, stuffing a dishevelled shirt tail into equally rumpled jeans and striding purposefully up the narrow hallway.

"You just passed the bathroom," yelled his mother, now in full pursuit. "Are you still asleep?"

"No, but I've got something to finish, I mean to do, first," Tim shouted back as he picked up the phone with one hand and started dialing with the other. A nervous few seconds lapsed before the first ring, then a second and a third ring and . . .

"Hello," said the friendly, mature female voice on the other end of the line.

"Hello Mrs. Turner. How are you? It's Nick White calling. Is Susan home?"

"Yes she is, Nick. Just one second."

The silence on the line was defeafening. Hunched over the phone and shifting his weight on crossed legs, Tim thought to himself: "I can't believe I'm actually doing this. I've got to stay focused now, but I should have gone to the toilet first. There are runners in scoring position . . ."

With a soft "hello" came the moment of truth. "Hi Susan. It's Nick White. Sorry about wrecking your chemistry experiment last week!"

"Don't worry about it, Nick. Accidents happen. The stains washed out of my blouse," Susan added with an audible laugh.

"I don't know why I tripped, but I'm glad you are not mad at me, Susan. By the way, did you go to the Prom last night?" Nick asked.

"Well, no, as it turned out," Susan replied. "I had hoped that maybe . . . well anyway, several of us girls who didn't have dates were going to go together, but then we thought that would look kind of stupid, so we didn't. How about you Nick. Did you go?"

"No, I didn't either. But I was just wondering if . . . Uh . . . Would you like to go to the movies with me tonight? Roman Holiday is playing with that new actress Audrey Hepburn," responded Nick without taking a breath for fear of breaking the verbal roll he was on.

"Wow, you've taken me by suprprise," gasped Susan, not completely believing what she had just heard. "Yes, I'd love to go Nick, but are you sure?"

"Trust me Susan, I'm sure! I'll be at your place at 7:00 o'clock sharp, so see you then. Thanks. Bye for now."

"Byeeee, Nick."

The flip flop of Nick's emotionally charged heart pulsating in the hollow of his chest, mixed with the drone of the telephone dial tone to create an almost orchestral rhythm in his ears. "We did it! Just as you said Dad," gushed an exuberant Nick glancing toward the heavens as he hung up the phone.

"Did you say something, Nick?" his mother asked over the sizzle of bacon frying on an open flame gas stove in the kitchen.

"No, nothing Mom," Nick replied, trying his best to sound nonchalant as he hurried down the hall toward the bathroom. A confident erectness replaced the previous slouch in his posture despite the fact that he was a young man answering an urgent call of nature. There was an immediate new spring in his step and a grin painted all over his beet-red face.

"Funny, but for a minute there I could have sworn that I felt your father's presence in the house. I even thought that I heard his laugh just as you hung up the telephone," continued his mother as she paused to wipe her hands on a freshly ironed gingham apron.

She was always philosophic about Nick's moods and stages being part of "the growing up process," but there was a surrealistic aura permeating the house this particular morning. With motherly instinct, she sensed that her Nicky had somehow experienced a mysterious metamorphose overnight and that it was very much for the better. She herself felt a sudden lifting of the parental aloneness that had been so heavy on her heart.

She was unable to explain any of it and she simply could not wait to hear what else Nick had to say about it.

"Oh, by the way, who were you talking to on the phone?" she asked, hoping to pry at least a clue out of her son.

"Awe, just a girl Mom. Susan Turner!"

From the old floor model Radio trope in the living room came the melodic strains of a hit song of the era, Got A Date With An Angel, performed by Skinny Ennis with his unmistakable breathy style.

"Got a date with an angel Got to meet her at seven Got a date with an angel And I'm on my way to heaven."

Nick pinched himself on the arm to make sure that this was not another one of his dreams.

"I'll explain everything in a few minutes, Mom!" he shouted with uncomfortable urgency, as the bathroom door slammed shut behind him.

The radio played on: "I've been waiting a lifetime For this evening at seven Got a date with an angel And I'm on my way to heaven."

NICK'S MOM: TRUE GRIT

WHEN NICK LEFT home to play baseball in the United States, his mother suffered the pangs of empty nest syndrome. Her husband did not leave her much more than the house and a few thousand dollars in life insurance when he died and she was forced to devote herself to fulltime employment in the local drug store.

She had a habit of complaining about assorted aches and pains, but somehow she managed to keep going. In later years Nick often wondered how long she would have lived past 92 if she had been fully healthy. She was strong-willed, extremely independent, and took exceptional pride in her work and personal appearance.

Characteristically thrifty, she was even able to save money from her Old Age and Canada Pension cheques after she quit working. If there was such a thing as loving a son too much, she was guilty as charged. In her mind Nick never passed 18 years of age and that presented a problem for mother and son at times. She had great expectations for Nick and she sacrificed a lot for him,

"I didn't show her enough appreciation at the time," lamented Nick. "When you are young you take a lot for granted. You don't really begin to appreciate parents until you become one yourself."

Mrs. White spent the last 20 years of her life feeling very lonely. Her comfort remained in the old home that had been the focal point of so many happy family gatherings in years gone by. So attached was she to her "cozy home" that Nick had to literally drag her into a nursing institution for the last four months of her life.

In the end, her strong will won out when she convinced Nick that she was well enough to go back home and he had no choice but to give in to her insistant pleas. Against his better judgement Nick reluctantly brought her home and she died five days later surrounded by all the things she loved—and all her memories.

Her last words to Nick were: "I'm so glad you listened to me for once, son." While Nick was second-guessed by friends and relatives, he would admit that he too was glad that he listened to his mother. "It was what my dad would have wanted me to do," he reasoned.

A few years earlier, on the occasion of her 89th birthday, she complained about her lack of a social life. A well-intended friend suggested that she join the local senior citizen's group because "they take bus trips, play euchre and hold regular dances."

The word "dances" seemed to trigger her ire. "Are you kidding? Me go to a dance and have some old foggy stumble up and ask me to dance?" she replied sharply with indignance written all over her face. In her mind, everybody else was old but her.

It was that spunky attitude and her pride that kept her going for all those years. It was also the reason that she felt that she did not belong in a nursing home, or "prison" as she called it. God bless her!

Meantime, with his baseball playing days behind him and a career in journalism beginning to unfold, Nick vowed to someday write about his mom and dad and growing up in a small town in the 1940s and 50s.

CHAPTER 2

WE LEARN FROM OUR FAILURES

S ECRETLY WE ALL harbor thoughts of failure, some stretching as far back as childhood. Ideally, we learn from the times when we have fallen short. There are cases, however, when we sustain wounds that tend to open when we are most vulnerable. A recent informal survey of friends and family revealed a general distaste for the word "failure", some going so far as to suggest that it be dropped completely from our vocabularies. Certainly failure represents our worst fears and is about as negative as you can get in terms of perception.

We do not have to like the word failure and all that it entails but care should be taken in closing the mind to it. One respondent put it this way: "I used to spend a lot of time avoiding failure. The good news was that I was able to achieve success at the end of the day. The bad news was that it was having a definite negative impact on my life. All effort to avoid failure caused me to be overly cautious and hesitant, even to the point of avoiding taking risks. Eventually I came to see failure as a form of education and the only real failure is if I stop trying."

A common first reaction to failure is to blame anyone and anything but ourselves. But if we perceive others are to blame then there is nothing we can do to correct the problem. We cannot change people's personalities, neither can they change ours. In assuming responsibility for the situation, however, we can analyze what went wrong and take corrective action. This approach is nothing more than the art of rebounding from failure. A single mother of two teenage daughters had this to say on the subject:

"The most important thing I have learned about failure is to take responsibility for it. I didn't for a long time—blaming others was easier. In discussing this whole issue with my daughters the other day they said that they know I feel regret over failures in my life, but they don't see it that way. In fact they revealed admiration for how I have handled things. I'm so impressed with their ability to understand and this is the single factor that now helps me get up in the morning."

Her experience was not unlike that of several others who agree that failure can simply be a matter of how one looks at a particular situation. A person who is only interested in the final outcome of an undertaking might well consider it to be a failure if the core issue was not resolved or a specific need not met.

"I can be very hard on myself, expecting perfection in most everything I do," said another young mother who has successfully combined professional life with responsibilities of homemaking for a family of five. "I look forward to a great end result, often rushing through a task just trying to get there. The fact that perfection, or desired outcome, is not always what I get does not necessarily discourage me because I see it as a learning experience. If you think about what it takes to achieve a successful end result—opportunity, knowledge, skill, a little luck—it is really amazing that any of us ever accomplish anything. I believe that if you gain something in any of these areas while working toward a goal, even if it's knowing your limits, the experience was not a failure."

She does not view "roads not traveled or doors not open" as failures because she does not believe she would be any happier in life had things gone differently. "It's both our successes and failures that make us who we are, but it's also in those not so great experiences that we learn the most about ourselves and grow stronger because of them," she adds philosophically.

From a very early age we are conditioned to scorn failure, the grading procedure in many of our school systems being the main culprit.—E for excellent, S for satisfactory, F for failure. The stigma of failure never completely leaves the mind of an impressionable young person and often leads to a deeply rooted complex in adulthood.

A 19-year-old university student refers to the "literal failure" of a test or class. "I think that there are two types of failure situations—one involving a learning experience and the other a failure in the true sense of the word," she explained. "Sadly, I am experiencing a lot of the latter where I have not studied for a test and did not learn a lesson from the experience, repeating the same mistake over and over again. That is true failure, in my mind.

Admittedly, my understanding of this concept is only a superficial one but at least I know what it is that I have to try to swing against in the near future."

A successful corporate banker, now retired, is one who truly dislikes the F-word, preferring instead "disappointment" because it seems a little less harsh. She alludes to the flip side being "for those who possess an abundance of self-confidence where the inner voice refuses to accept that they could, or might, fail." Here's her story.

"My dream was always to be a nurse. It didn't happen for various reasons. My substitute career was banking which took me further than I ever expected but down deep it was never what I wanted. Consequently I turned down some opportunities to aspire to higher positions. Why? Was I angry with myself? Inwardly annoyed that I wasn't doing what I wanted? Afraid that I didn't really have the know-how to play in the corporate world? Afraid of failure?

"Ah, finally, confession that the word does exist in my world."

In retirement she is finally in a hospital environment as a one-day-a-week volunteer which is a far lesser role than she originally planned for herself. But with that limited exposure she now sees the potential that existed for her in the health care field.

"I could have broadened my dream and been a doctor, a specialist or researcher," she says in retrospection. "My inner regret/slash failure is that I didn't just suck it up and push myself through. How true it is that with age comes not only wisdom but sometimes the confidence we lacked when younger. So, it is best for me to not reflect on the 'what ifs' but rather accept 'what was (is)' and thank God that I have succeeded just a little . . ."

Then we have a respondent who refuses altogether to consider the possibility of failure. "Remaining positive is very important in my line of work. I try very hard to eliminate anything negative from my day-to-day functions and that includes any thoughts of failure.

Success is the 'buy' word," the career salesman adds with a laugh that fails to mask completely his commitment to the oft recited play on words.

Rejection, or failure to close a sale, rolls off a bonifide salesperson like water off a duck's back.

Not too surprisingly, 50 per cent of those contacted for this article chose not to comment. It is not easy to open up about failure. For some it is simply not a comfortable subject.

Personally, I confess to being failure conscious and living in the past a little more than may be in my best interest. I have a habit of going to bed at night replaying the "what if" reel of disappointment and failure in my life. Just recently I have taken to repeating to myself a line from the movie Sybil: "The past is the present if you hold on to it." This seeems to help me return to the reality of where I am now in life and being thankful for how I got here.

There is a lot to be said for the idea of letting go. Pining over the past is really an exercise in futility, especially when it has so little to offer. If you examine your situation carefully and objectively, you will realize that certain things have to happen, generally for the better.

Regardless of how we look at failure, it is a fact of life and the sooner we rationalize it the better it is for us. It is even better when, in turn, we pick ourselves up, dust ourselves off, and get on with reclaiming our life and all that it has to offer.

Here's another personal story about a perceived failure in my life and how it took many years to rationalize it.

FAILURE IS IN THE EYE OF THE BEHOLDER

Take it from a 1.000 hitter!

"FAILURE" IS AN abstract noun that in general refers to the state, or condition, of not meeting a desirable or intended objective. It is the opposite of success. It has taken a long time but I have come to realize that the criteria for failure are heavily dependent on context of use and may be relative to a particular observer or belief mind set. A situation considered to be a failure by one individual might well be deemed a success by another.

Failure reared its ugly head for me early and often in my formative years but an ironic twist to one of the more hurtful situations has been amusingly healing for me, 50 years after the fact.

Not long ago I had occasion to be in contact with Jay-Dell Mah who has created a most remarkable web site reflecting on semi-professional baseball on the Canadian Prairies in the heydays of the 1940s and 50s. As a result of our initial exchange, Jay asked me about my baseball background and how it evolved over the years. In response, among other things, I recalled my brief stint as a professional baseball player in 1956.

As a pitching prospect, I attended a baseball tryout in Cocao, Florida and eventually signed a minor league contract with the Washington Senators on my 18th birthday. I was assigned to the independent Donalsonville, Georgia, Seminoles of the Florida-Alabama League.

The pitcher of record in an exhibition game victory over the Florida State University team, I was slated to "start" the Seminoles' third game of the regular season league schedule. "Ontario (me) is starting tonight," manager Neb Wilson seemed to warn my teammates in a pre-game huddle . . ."So be on your toes!"

The opposing shortstop connected with my first pitch and sent it 400 feet over the fence in centre field. "Relax kid. You're as pale as a ghost", was the best that Neb could offer as he met me on the mound. I managed to survive another three innings in the game before being relieved with our team trailing by a 3-1 margin. Happily we rallied in the 7th inning and ended up winning the game.

Much to my surprise I was called on to pinch hit in a game several nights later and I managed to bang out a single. Boy, that one really felt good. A much needed boost to my confidence, albeit temporary.

Still feeling very full of myself with my batting prowess, I could not wait to get to the ball park the next night. Several steps inside the club house door I was stopped dead in my tracks. Someone was sitting at my locker, putting on my uniform.

"Better talk to the manager" offered the crew cut stranger, but I didn't have to. The sickening, insensitive message was clear. I was being cut from the team roster. Lost and deflated, I left the ball park. Couldn't face staying to watch the game.

"Survival of the fittest," I was told next day as I picked up my pay cheque and outright release papers. It was explained that I and several others were being dropped from the team to make room for players from the higher class Provincial League that had suspended operations the previous week.

A dream dashed. I was "washed up" at 18 years of age and there was nothing to do but to return home to Canada—in my mind, a failure. Although I went on to enjoy quite a few years as a semi-pro and amateur player, that experience and the hurt of it all left me with an unhealthy complex for the next five-plus decades. That is until I received an email from my new electronic friend Jay, Subject: "A note of a 1,000 hitter as a professional".

Jay had taken it upon himself to resource the Minor Baseball Leagues Data Base where he miraculously turned up my statistical record for the all-too-brief season of 1956. I had no idea such records existed. I was dumbfounded. But there it was in black and white, for posterity: "Richard Wright, FABL, Donalsonville Seminoles, pitching 0-0; hitting 1-1, pct. 1,000."

In his email message to me Jay made no mention of my sad record as a pitcher, choosing instead to highlight my perfect record as a hitter in the pros. He did not see me as the failure I had perceived for all those years. He even went so far as write a piece about me on his web site, referring to my "oh so short" pro ball experience and the fact that I got a hit in my "only time at bat". I guess Jay thought he was doing me a favor but, personally, my first impulse was to think that he had published just a little too much information.

It's a bit of a stretch but, come to think of it, I can legitimately boast of being a "1,000 hitter as a pro". I never thought of it that way before. Very few other former ball players, if any, can make such a claim and if that is not a positive spin, I do not know what is. It kind of feels good too, in a strange sort of way.

The message: There is a positive in every negative. You just have to look for it! But, like yours truly, don't wait for 50 years to have someone else find it for you.

CHAPTER 3

OVER TO A NEW GENERATION
OF GARDENERS

S OMEONE MUCH WISER than me once said that to see any
question clearly, go far from it and study the picture as though you
had no place in it. My old friend and role model Arthur Brisbane used
imaginary outer terrestrials in that way to view life on earth for his literary
pruposes.

Suppose, just for a moment, that you were one of Brisbane's superior beings
from another planet looking at this earth with its rivers, mountains, trees,
lush green fields and millions of human beings scattered over its surface.
The earth no doubt would look like a great garden in need of cultivation
and you would see the little microscopic, two-legged human creatures as
gardeners or caretakers. If you were asked "Why were the little humans put
on the planet?" you would probably explain:

"God created the beautiful planet and he takes extreme pride in it. He puts
little creatures there to cultivate the surface, drain the marshes, irrigate
the deserts, and finally make a glorious and beautiful park of the whole
earth."

You might also add that you marvel at His patience with the little humans,
often called people, that fight each other and rob and cheat and waste their
time with self-serving tasks instead of working on the great garden confided
to their care.

Who today can doubt that the great power of Law and Justice that rules the
universe and maintains it in perpetual equilibrium and warm sunlight, has
failed to plan for the fullest development of the spark of cosmic consciousness
called soul which is the mainspring in each of us. The destiny of the planet,

born in heat and fire and changing through long millions of years, was ultimately to be an ideal home, perfect and beautiful.

One thing the NASA spece program has shown us is that no other planet in the solar system is likely to have life as we know it, surrounded by the beauty of nature that we so often take for granted.

The human race, emerging from ignorance, passing through hundreds of thousands of years of suffering, struggling, poverty, ferocious combat, famine and disease has, in truth, attained a marvelous degree of civilization and knowledge but the wonderful future that was to be its reward is in serious jeopardy as we move along into the 21st century. True brotherhood to live happily on this planet has not been achieved. For the most part, we have been sloppy gardeners.

Man's inhumanity to man is rife. The threat of world-wide terror has never been greater. We are constantly at war, losing the lives of our young "defenders of peace" in a terrible way and at an astronomical cost. To compound matters, we have ingnorantly and carelessly damaged the ecological system, almost to the point of no return. Governments are motivated by votes and not always by the best interests of the voters. We are on a slippery slope and not moving in the right direction. Sadly, figuratively and realistically, we are losing ground.

The human gardener needs to take a serious look back and another proactive look forward. We need to engage in some honest self-questioning and self-reproach before we lose complete control of the garden that was entusted to us. Pray that it is not too late to make restitution and to resume the care taking role that seems to have been abandoned out of ignorance and human shortsightedness.

Without question, if this was a test we would fail. There is precious little time to achieve a passing grade, but it is possible with help in the form of the young ones we currently feed, clothe and send off to school each day.

Honestly, the hope of humanity as a race rests ultimately with a new generation of gardeners—a generation that has learned from our mistakes and is prepared to do whatever is necessary to restore, and then maintain, the beauty and harmony that can exist in this big green garden for centuries to come. Maybe it starts with societal benevolence, helping those in need to get back on their feet and to become productive stewards of the garden in their own right.

So there you go, young people. If you have been wondering what to do with your life, here is a big challenge for you. Please understand that you are more than just a drop in the ocean of humanity and it is going to take all of you, pulling together, to push the garden forward as its creator intended. My generation of gardeners regrets having to leave you with this huge responsibility, but for better or worse, it is your destiny . . . Here's to good gardening!

CHAPTER 4

LITTLE THINGS, BIG REALITY

I HAVE ALWAYS been fascinated by the value of small or little things in life and hold to the conviction that "small things mean a lot". It is interesting how small things can have huge impacts. Also, can you truthfully think of anything that is not made up of small parts?

Think of the "parts" in our bodies for instance, and coral rock that is the work of tiny insects; the number of peas in a peck; the number of pennies in a dollar; stars in the universe; rain drops in a storm; grains of sand on a beach; blades of grass in a lawn; notes in a song; words in a book; people in a crowd—we could go on forever. If you really want to blow your mind, just start thinking in terms of molecules and atoms.

Little things, too, can affect us physically like the tiny nerve of a tooth that can sometimes drive us to distraction or any one of thousands of microscopic germs that can make us deathly ill. Think of the poor elephant that is driven absolutely mad by a tiny speck of a mosquito.

Moments are the golden sands of time. Every day is a little life and our whole life is but a day repeated. A word, a look, a frown are all little things, but they can have powerful impact for good and evil.

There is no denying that little acts are the elements of true greatness. They raise life's value, like little figures over the larger ones in arithmetic, to its higher power. Small things in youth accumulate into character in age and destiny in eternity. A novelist who writes a book must do it sentence by sentence. A student of science must master it fact by fact and principle by principle.

Happiness in life is made up of little courtesies, little kindnesses, pleasant words, genial smiles, self-assuring touches, hugs, good wishes and good deeds, acts of charity. It is by studying small things that we attain the great art of having as little misery and as much happiness as possible in journeying through life.

It is the little things that, in aggregate, make up the whole of whatever is great. That is what fascinates me so much because little things are all I have to offer the world, and maybe that is not so bad after all.

CHAPTER 5

FEATHER HAD SPECIAL MEANING: AN OMEN ON A RAILWAY TRACK

F EATHERS HAVE DIFFERENT meanings for different people. To some they are reminders of angel wings, to others they are dream catchers or representative of mythology, religion or magic. In practical applications, feathers have been used for writing and in masks, pillows, comforters, all forms of art, dusters, hats and even in fly fishing lures.

For me, personally, feathers have an almost spiritual significance, spanning a life time. Here's how it all started.

INSPIRATIONAL FEATHER

I was a struggling young novice newspaper reporter trudging along the New York Central Railroad tracks in St. Thomas, Ontario, on a warm July day in 1961. I was feeling very sorry for myself after an editor had rejected as so much "garbage" a story I had written 45 minutes earlier. "I left my job in the clothing store for this aggravation? Maybe I'm not a writer after all. I'm wasting my time. I should just quit," I sobbed unashamedly.

Absorbed in the misery of self-doubt, I was totally oblivious to my surroundings. I paused to kick a stone off a railroad tie and realized that, instead, I had disturbed a large feather. It was a perfect specimen of unknown origin and something about it made me pick it up as I turned and headed back to the newspaper office, my future as a journalist very much in doubt.

As I approached the front door of The Times-Journal, I paused to drop the feather into a trash can but it was as if it was stuck to my fingers. I couldn't let it go. "Oh well, maybe I'll keep it for now," I reasoned as I entered the building.

I was greeted by a familiar gravely voice from behind a desk in the advertising department: "Hey Wright, what's that you've got there? Is editorial giving you quill pens to write with now?"

"Very funny," I mumbled, not appreciating the humor of the moment.

Dejectedly mounting the stairs to the second floor newsroom, the words "quill pen" echoed in my ears. As I looked down at the 12-inch feather clutched in my hand, I had to agree that it did look something like an old quill pen that had its origin in the 17th century. A literary symbol to be sure. "Could this be an omen of some kind? Is there a message for me here?" I wondered.

Tucking the feather into my shirt pocket, I hurried to my desk and jammed a handful of copy paper into the trusty 1920s vintage Underwood typewriter that I had inherited from the dozens of reporters before me. For the next 30 minutes I hammered out a rewrite of the previously rejected story. The sudden free flow of thoughts and words was amazing as I applied the required inverted pyramid style of news writing for perhaps the first time.

"That's more like it, Dickie boy!" remarked the city editor upon a quick scan of my second effort just minutes shy of deadline. "Why didn't you write it this way in the first place?"

When the newspaper rolled off the press that afternoon, my story was prominently displayed on the front page of the second section. I had officially arrived as a newspaper reporter. I never again questioned my ability to write, thanks to that old feather which remains a source of creative inspiration for me to this day.

A gift from God? . . . I think so!

MY LITTLE FEATHER GIRL

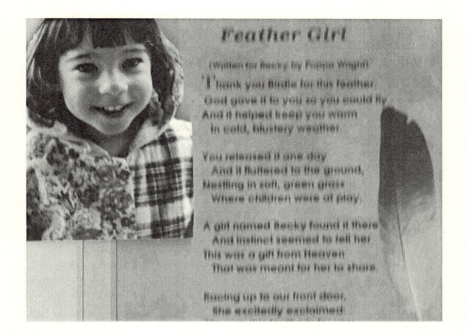

Feather Girl

(Written for Becky by Poppa Wright)

Thank you Birdie for this feather,
God gave it to you so you could fly
And it helped keep you warm
In cold, blustery weather.

You released it one day
And it fluttered to the ground,
Nestling in soft, green grass
Where children were at play.

A girl named Becky found it there
And instinct seemed to tell her
This was a gift from Heaven
That was meant for her to share.

Racing up to our front door,
She excitedly exclaimed

BECKY HAD BUILT-IN RADAR FOR FEATHERS

THE MEANING OF feathers in my life was never more graphically reinforced than through a surrealistic experience involving my then three-year-old granddaughter Becky. It was a quiet late spring morning and I was enjoying my second cup of coffee over the newspaper at the kitchen table.

"Poppa, I find 'dis for you!" an excited Beck shouted as she burst through our front door with a tiny white feather gingerly balanced in the palm of her chubby outstretched hand. "Thank you Becky. Where did you find it?" I asked.

"In your front yard and there's whole lot more," was her enthusiastic reply. "Come on. I show you!"

Sure enough, upon inspection, we found four more identical feathers clumped together in the grass under a small tree. I thought to myself: "Poor little bird lost most of its tail feathers so that we could have a message of some description?"

Coincidentally, within that very hour I was scheduled to attend a meeting with three young artists who were putting together a special exhibit designed to spread the message of God in a native perspective for First Nations youth. A feather, as First Nations legend has it, represents a message from the spirit world and is considered to be a gift from The Creator.

I placed Becky's feathers in a plastic bag and, with her approval, took it to the meeting. When I showed the feathers to my artist friends they were ecstatic. To them it was an indication that their project was receiving God's blessing. Extremely encouraged, the group decided on the spot to incorporate the name "The Plume Society" and Becky was adopted as their "Feather Girl".

"Yep, I'm the Feather Girl," Becky would say, relentless in living up to her new name and keeping her Poppa the benefactor of her keen eye for finding feathers—dozens of them in ensuing years in fact. At one point, from a distance of more than 100 yards, she spotted a black feather on the grave of her grandmother who had passed away several weeks earlier. Leaving others in amazement, she raced to the feather and carefully placed it on the head stone. Go figure!

I was so impressed with what had transpired that I penned the following poem:

Feather Girl

Thank you birdie for this feather
God gave it to you so you could fly
And it helped keep you warm
In cold, blustery weather.

You released it one day,
It fluttered to the ground
Nestling in soft, green grass
Where children were at play.

A girl named Becky found it there
And instinct seemed to tell her
It was a gift from the Heavens
Meant for her to share.

Racing up to our front door
She excitedly exclaimed:
"Poppa, this feather's for you
And I'll find many more!"

So you see, gentle Dove,
How a tradition was born,
And we now have a Feather Girl
Who's a messenger of love.

GIVING FLIGHT TO BECKY'S FEATHERS

AWARE OF MY growing feather collection, thanks to my granddaughter Becky the "Feather Girl" who made contributions almost daily, a friend passed on to me a clipping from an issue of Prevention Magazine. In this article, author/publisher Ardath Rodale shared a tender part of her life after the tragic deaths of her husband and son in an automobile accident.

Mrs. Rodale explained that after the loss of her loved ones she felt very much alone, particularly at holiday times. Often she wondered how she could cope without them, and she would cry out: "Please let me know that you are with me! What should I do?"

"I never got the what to do reply, but I have gotten the we are here with you message," she wrote. That message came in the form of feathers which she said she now finds wherever she goes, even though she does not always consciously look for them. "With each feather I feel that Bob and David are with me from up in the heavens and seeing me grow stronger every day . . . They have become my heavenly cheerleaders," she added.

She also believed that her feathers were given to her as a spiritual gift and that she had begun to add to her life the dimension of the "potlatch" or give-away ceremony traditionally celebrated by First Canadians on the west coast of British Columbia. She now gives her treasured feathers to others with special needs, in the hope that they too might be lifted in spirit.

"What a wonderful idea," I thought. "Now I know what I'm going to do with Becky's feathers." Between the two of us at one point several years ago, I had amassed a collection of more than 70 feathers of all shapes, colors and sizes.

The first opportunity to begin my feather give-away in a major way came one Sunday morning when I was guest speaker at a church service in Port Elgin. Appropriately, the theme on that particular Sunday was "The Joy of Giving" and I ended my talk by telling the "Feather Girl Story". At the conclusion of the service I gave out feathers to just about everyone in attendance—69 in total, according to my recapitulation. I later heard from a number of individuals who were in the congregation that day who said that they, in turn, had given their feathers to others. Mission accomplished!

To this day I cannot pass a feather without picking it up. I have them in my house, in my garage, in my car and in my wallet. Becky's production has dropped off recently, a natural evolution of a 17-year-old girl who has a busy social calendar and a demanding school itinerary, not to mention changing priorities in her life. One of her more recent gifts to me, however, just happens to be in the form of a quill pen, ball-point variety. I'll never give that one away!

Times change, people's lives evolve, but God's gifts remain constant . . . They come down from above for us every day. We don't have to look for them nor ask for them. All we have to do is just pick them up—and share them.

I'm luckier than most. I've had the gift of a Feather Girl in my life. Now I'm about to share her with the world too.

CHAPTER 6

THE MAGIC OF PLAYING SANTA

SANTA ME AND GRANDDAUGHTER ALYSSA

ONE THING I'VE missed about Christmas the past few years is playing Santa Claus. Once you've immersed yourself into the role of the Jolly Old Gent on a legitimate basis, you take on an entirely new perspective of the greatest of all traditional myths.

Not everyone can be a realistic Santa, or a Santa's helper, depending on the dictates of the occasion. It takes someone with a light heart and a genuine love of children, who himself has never really fully grown up. Most importantly, to make the transformation believable, one has to be the biggest type of ham imaginable and a bit of a thespian to boot.

Over the years I have played Santa Claus in just about every possible setting and venue—Sunday School concerts, hospitals, children's parties, company staff parties, community parades and in major city shopping centres. One of my most memorable experiences as Santa came when I skated out onto arena ice and into a swarm of 200 screaming junior figure skaters ages four to 10 (see attached photo clipping from The St. Thomas Times-Journal). No question about it, there were a few minutes of sheer panic as I struggled helplessly on my blades against the force of kid power which let up only when we crushed into the boards at the opposite end of the ice.

In the photo I can be seen with granddaughter Alyssa, then 3 (now 20 and a university student), sitting on my lap at the City Centre in Bramalea. Alyssa was at first reluctant but she eventually warmed up to the visit when she seemed to detect something strangely familiar about this particular Santa.

Once you don a Santa suit, wig, beard and an appropriate amount of strategically-placed padding, you actually lose your identity and any lingering inhibitions. You magically become Santa Claus, saying and doing things that you never would under normal conditions when stripped of the velvety crimson costume and snow white beard. It is a rush like none other, leaving you completely drained on one hand, but totally exhilarated on the other.

Kids, of course, are always great. The look of wonder on their faces makes it all worthwile. There's a down side, however—upset stomachs, dirty diapers and excessive terrified crying and kicking can test the staying power of even the heartiest Santa. Surprisingly, teenagers and adults of both sexes and all ages are the ones that really surprise you. I've had them all sit on my knee (I should say Santa's knee) and be reduced to the giddy, squirming child they used to be. Hugs and kisses, too, were not unusual. Santa just has that amazing affect on everyone.

It goes without saying that the best way to break the ice with a shy youngster is to ask what they want for Christmas. But you have to be prepared for the odd surprise answer that leaves you struggling to keep your composure. I have never forgotten one very serious little guy who responded to my stock query: "I'd like world peace, Santa!" Then there was the sad-eyed little girl who quietly replied "I'd like my mommy and daddy to get back together." God bless them. Santa could only pray for Devine Intervention.

There are some common do's and dont's that I would pass on to all aspiring Santas, such as:

- always go to the washroom before putting on the costume
- don't drink liquids before an appearance
- do kids a favor, don't eat garlic or onions 24 hours before an appearance
- before making your grand entrance prepare your mindset by thinking "jovial" thoughts—kids overlook a lot of flaws if Santa is kind, caring and jovial—its all about having fun
- be careful with the placement of your hands when a child is on your lap
- never make promises that Santa (or parents) can't keep
- never make references to mom or dad—you just never know
- memorize the names of all Santa's reindeer
- play the role realistically, minimize forced HO HO HOs and remember that Santa's laugh comes naturally from deep within his ample belly
- always pre-test the tug ability of the elastic on your beard

All in all, just a wonderful experience, but I always felt that it was a good thing that Christmas only comes once a year . . . It takes that long for Santa to recuperate.

CHAPTER 7

I WAS A FIGURE SKATING DAD

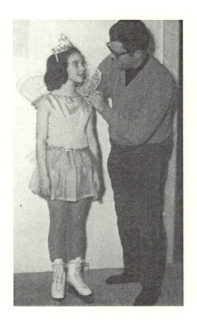

ADJUSTING DEBBIE'S FAIRY WINGS FOR THE BIG SHOW

THIS IS ONE of my favorite stories as a Dad who found himself "growing up" with his daughters. It was published originally in The St. Thomas Times-Journal, March 1970.

It is not easy being the father of a figure skating daughter. It takes patience, nerves of steel, understanding and—most important of all—an adjustment that is certain to change your entire outlook on life.

For a dad who has devoted much of his existence to playing, coaching and writing about sports and envisioning one day watching his own son pitch a no-hitter in baseball or lead his hockey team to a crucial overtime victory, the adjustment to figure skating dad does not come overnight.

The change in you begins with the concession that the dream of having a sports star for a son is not likely to materialize and you had better start making the best of the two wonderful daughters you have been blessed with. That much is easy, really.

The part that eats away at you in the beginning is that you actually find yourself becoming involved in things you never imagined you would . . . And strangely enjoying it.

Take the aforementioned figure skating for instance. I must confess that I exposed my eight-year-old daughter Debbie to this form of winter activity on an organized basis for the first time a year ago. "She'll enjoy it, and who knows, maybe she will be the Barbara Anne Scott of the future," I reasoned. (There I go again, dreaming.) Trouble is, I didn't know what I was letting myself in for.

It is painful to recall my first experience at taking Debbie to the arena for an introductory figure skating session. The thought that figure skating is "sissy stuff", deep-rooted since boyhood, suddenly came back to me as we made our way down the arena corridor, hand-in-hand.

"Golly, I hope I don't run into anyone I know," I thought as I turned up my coat collar and entered a dressing room marked "Ladies" to help Debbie lace up her skates.

My first encounter with a figure skating club official threw me for yet another loop. "Is this your daughter's first year?" I was asked. "It is? Well then as a junior she . . ." What followed was a rapid-fire litany of information completely confusing to me.

"Are there any questions?" I was finally asked. "No", I lied, suddenly reduced from the sports authority I thought I was to a red-faced, novice figure skating parent.

The months that followed were filled with ups and downs for both father and daughter. It was sheer torture at first. I swear it hurt me more than it did her every time she fell on the ice. When she was mastering a certain step or figure, my heart ached for her, and when she did well the pride swelled within me almost to the point of shouting for all to hear: "That's my daughter out there!"

Between lessons and patches we would work on routines together at home and on the more spacious Pinafore Pond ice surface where we could stretch out, many evenings long after dark. I learned from first-hand experience the difficulty in keeping edges and performing figure 8s. The Dutch Waltz was a particular challenge for both of us but eventually we got the hang of it—Debbie good enough that she passed her all-important dance test (skating with the reigning Canadian juvenile pairs champion as her partner certainly did not harm her cause).

The Carnival: Biggest Test of All

The experiences of those developing months were nothing, however, compared to what was to come in the form of the annual figure skating carnival—The Big Show.

"Similar carnivals marking the end of the figure skating season are held in almost every arena in Canada at this time of year," I tried to convince myself, "and they haven't lost a figure skating parent yet."

So wrapped up was I by this time that I didn't even flinch when it was announced that my daughter had been selected as a "fairy" in the show. But as the carnival date drew near I began to experience a new type of anxiety and the night of the production I was so much on edge I could hardly even finish my second helping of mashed potatoes.

"Aren't you just a little nervous?" I asked Debbie, misery enjoying company. "Nope, not really," she replied . . ."Can I have some more chocolate pudding?"

The events of the next few hours are not completely clear, but I noticed later that somehow my finger nails had been bitten to the quick. We were two blocks from the arena when my wife Anne had the presence of mind to ask

If I had picked up the carnival tickets from the kitchen table. After a return trip home, we arrived at the arena along with some 2,500 other people.

As I sat in my hard, cold arena seat waiting for the show to begin and wiping beads of perspiration from my forehead, I could not help but think how far the two of us had come in the past few months—Debbie as a skater and I as a father.

The lights dimmed and the music began—the big moment was at hand. When Debbie finally skated onto the ice with 19 other daintily attired youngsters, I had a lump in my throat and an ache in the pit of my stomach. I noticed a tear hovering in the corner of my wife's eye.

The Fairies performed to perfection and if any of them made mistakes we didn't notice. It wouldn't have mattered anyway.

When the Fairies skated off the ice to a thunderous applause that had its density in our section of the arena, it was as if a great weight had been lifted from my shoulders.

Yes, it isn't easy being the father of a figure skating daughter, but I'm a battle-scarred veteran now. I'll be in better shape for next season when my younger daughter Cindy takes to the figure skating ice for the first time. I'm looking forward to it!

IT ALL STARTED ON BACKYARD RINKS

Debbie and Cindy learned to skate on back yard rinks that I would flood by hand (countless buckets of water and frozen fingers and toes). Cindy had exceptionally fat, wide feet and actual figure skates were out of the question in the beginnng. I purchased the smallest pair of boys hockey skates that I had ever seen from a skate exchange and Cindy took to them immediately. When she was ready to graduate to figure skates the next winter she had to learn to skate all over again. I prized those little hockey skates and years later I made bookends out of them. A fitting "trophy" for a former figure skating dad.

CHAPTER 8

BOY WHO MADE A BIG CATCH

WHAT GARY LACKED in baseball talent he more than made up for in determination. This is a story about "giving a kid a chance" even though he may not be the second coming of the great Mickey Mantle.

I could not ignore the sullen, pensive face of the teenager sitting alone in the stands behind home plate. Handing a fungo bat over to an assistant coach, I made my way to where the young lad was sitting.

Seeing me approaching, he quickly shoved a dilapidated old baseball glove behind his back on the bleacher seat, as if hiding it from my view. "Are you here to try out?" I asked him.
    "No, I guess not," he replied with hesitation.

"Well I noticed you have a glove with you and you're welcome to join the guys on the field if you like," I said in return. Without taking his eyes off the activity on the diamond he repeated, "No thanks, I don't think so."

"Okay, it's up to you. What's your name anyway and how old are you?" I quizzed further. "I'm Gary and I'm 14," was the answer.

"Well, maybe we'll see you again Gary, but if you change your mind . . ." I was interrupted in mid-sentence with the almost inaudible: "I'm not very good!"

"I was not asking how good you are, Gary . . . Look, I have to get back to the field, but stick around and after we're finished the practice I would like to see just how 'not very good' you really are," I added rather sharply.

It took close to an hour to complete the mid-season drills I was conducting with the minor baseball bantam team I was coaching at the time. As the players were changing their spikes and gathering up equipment, I noticed Gary had moved a little closer to the dugout with his hand now stuffed awkwardly in his baseball glove.

"Hey Gary," I shouted. "Come on in and we'll play a little catch."

"Okay," he said, slowly making his way around the backstop screen. "But remember, I'm not very good."

My first 40-foot toss to the lanky teen hit him squarely in the chest without even touching his glove. His return throw to me sailed a good three feet over my head.

Gary was right. He was not very good.

Not wanting to prolong the agony, I invited him to sit down for a chat. In the ensuing conversation I learned that Gary's father had died of a sudden heart attack when he was only 11 years old, a story eerily similar to mine. He lived with his elderly grandmother, mother and younger sister. He always wanted to play baseball but the opportunity never presented itself.

Touched by his story, I suggested that I was willing to work with Gary individually for a week or two and that he might even be able to join the team at some stage. He seemed to be encouraged by the prospect.

Quite frankly, I did not know what I was letting myself in for. It would be a painful period that was in store for the two of us, literally and figuratively.

Gary would join me for one-on-one workouts whenever I could manage the time. We played catch and pepper primarily, just to get him comfortable with fielding and making contact with the bat. After the third session he was actually catching one of five fly balls I was hitting to him from a distance of about 90 feet.

After several weeks he was showing enough improvement that I felt it would do no harm to expose him to team practices. He was beginning to bond with the other players (I guess they did not feel threatened by him) and I thought, what the heck, why not let him sit on the bench for our final three games of the season. I even scrapped up a make-do uniform for him.

I could not help but notice that Gary was starting to walk a lot taller. He showed up for our final game pounding his fist into a brand new Spalding Pro glove purchased by his mother at an end-of-season clearance sale.

The team jumped to an early three-run lead in the game and added a couple of insurance runs in the 5th inning. That's when I started to toy with the dangerous idea of putting Gary out in right field to start the 7th and final inning. After all, we had a safe five-run lead over the visiting team . . . didn't we?

In the bottom of the 6th I pondered in earnest the pros and cons of letting Gary into the game and finally threw caution to the wind. I just thought I owed it to him after all his hard work and dedication.

"You're in right field," I announce to the figure sitting at the end of the bench. "Me? Are you sure?" replied an obviously shocked Gary. "No," I barked back, "and if you don't move now I'm apt to change my mind."

I was proud and nauseous, all at the same time, as I watched him lope out onto the field cradling his new glove and stopping at second base to pull up socks that had fallen down around his ankles. I pretended not to hear a few moans and negative comments from the stands.

Our up-to-then flawless pitcher managed to retire the first batter in the 7th, but then the roof started to cave in. An infield single, followed by two walks and an RBI out to centre gave the opposition its first run in the game. A second run scored on a passed ball. Another walk and a scratch single loaded the bases again.

Just like that, our once comfortable lead was in jeopardy. I simply crossed my fingers and refused to think of what fate might have in store for us with the tying run on first base and the potential go-ahead run at the plate. Adding pressure to the moment was the up-to-now forgotten fact that first place in the final league standings was resting on the outcome of the game.

As luck would have it, the next batter was a left hand hitter and I had a lefty throwing in the bull pen. I called time, went to the mound and congratulated my starting pitcher on doing so well for us. Assuring him that we would preserve the win, I took the ball and made the pitching change.

Our relief pitcher worked a 2-2 count on the batter and suspense mounted in the ball park. The next pitch was just a little inside and the batter took a healthy cut at it, lofting the ball high into (you guessed it) right field where Gary was camped.

Gary took a couple of steps forward and then a whole bunch of them quickly backward, stumbling in the process. The ball seemed to be suspended in the cloudless blue sky. My heart stopped completely.

As the ball descended, Gary seemed to be surrounding it. He raised his new Spalding Pro in stiff-arm fashion and PLOP! the ball hit in the webbing and miraculously stayed there. GAME OVER!

His teammates stormed into right field and mobbed Gary, hoisting him to their shoulders. The hometown crowd went wild. The hero for this day pumped his fist and waved vigorously in acknowledgement.

When the celebrations subsided, Gary broke away from the crowd and made his way over to me. We hugged. "Thanks for everything!" he said. That was all I needed to hear. I was momentarily speechless. There was a lump in my throat that stopped anything from coming out.

This was one of those priceless special occasions that make the time and effort spent in coaching all worthwhile.

I moved away a short time later and lost track of Gary. I wonder where he is today and if he remembers?

CHAPTER 9

CANCER: HOW WE SURVIVED

S EVERAL WEEKS BEFORE my wife Anne would succumb to the ravages of cancer, she suggested that I "should write a story about our experiences because it might be helpful for other couples". It was the first and only time that she would ask that I write anything. She had always been blase about my literary efforts. Recognizing the urgency in her voice, I acted on her wishes and submitted copy to The Toronto Star. Unfortunately, The Star only used excerpts from my story in an article carrying the byline of a staff writer. Disappointed, I just filed away the text with some other unpublished material. In memory of Anne and as a tribute to her spirit and strength over an extremely difficult nine-year struggle with cancer, I hereby fulfill her wishes with the following revised and updated version of the original story that had her blessing before she passed away.

MY FAVORITE PHOTO, HONEYMOON 1960

W. ANNE WRIGHT, 1940-2000

. . . mother, banker, friend, free spirit

For several months I had been noticing something different about my wife Anne—subtle things like uncharacteristic evasiveness, a change in her posture, the way she would position herself in bed at night, her declining energy level and a far away look in her eyes. There were also husband and wife issues developing between us that I could not explain. I was reluctant to ask questions, because I was afraid of what the answers might be. The answer, however, came in bolt of lightening fashion one Monday morning in May, 1991, as we were getting dressed for work.

Generally the first one dressed and downstairs preparing coffee, Anne was dragging herself at a snail's pace. When I had to help her from the bathroom into the bedroom, I knew we had a problem. "That's it," I said firmly. "You are not going to work this morning and I'm going to call the doctor." Anne collapsed into a chair and with a weak voice said: "Okay, but maybe you should have a look at something before we go."

"Do you think you can handle it?" she asked as she shifted her brassier to reveal to me for the first time an ugly red mass about the size of a baseball right in the middle of her chest. I felt faint and gasped the obvious question: "My God, how long have you had it?"

"I'm embarrassed to admit it, but I first noticed something about a year ago. I didn't say anything because I kept hoping it would go away. I wanted to spare you the anguish because all I can think of is what we went through with my mother when she died of cancer," she confessed.

I could not believe what I was seeing and hearing. I actually pinched myself just in case I was dreaming. We sat on the edge of the bed, minds racing, saying nothing, crying. Anne finally broke the silence. "You know, I actually feel like a great weight has been lifted. I don't have to keep this a secret any more . . . No more hiding it . . . No more pretending."

The worry and stress that she kept bottled up all those months was beyond comprehension. I more or less understood why she decided to ignore early detection signs, but a wave of guilt came over me because rather than confide in me, she chose to shut me out. How insensitive of me not to have put two and two together.

Four hours later, seated in his office, our family doctor gave Anne a hug and confirmed our worst fears. It was the first time that we gave in to the nasty C-word. Our lives would never be the same again. For the next nine-plus years we would literally and figuratively be consumed by the most insidious of diseases—cancer.

At 51 years of age, Anne was supposed to be in the prime of her life. She had a fulfilling career in banking and had successfully raised two fine daughters. Now this. Our world as we knew it had just crumbled around us and we were about to embark on a journey that would test our commitment, our strength and our resolve.

Anne was immediately referred to an oncologist at Peel Memorial Hospital in Brampton. After preliminary tests and a hastily arranged mammogram, it was determined that her cancer had advanced to the inoperable stage, leaving chemotherapy as the only treatment option. The cancer was starting to engulf her left breast and was also showing up in her lungs. Her long-term prognosis was not good, but the oncologist told her that he could "buy" her at least a year of good quality time.

For the next five months she would endure bi-weekly chemotherapy drips as a hospital outpatient. From the very first treatment she was extremely sick. She would come home from the hospital completely drained and sleep for most of the next 24 hours. It would take five or six days for her to regain her strength and then it would be time for another treatment. It was a cruel, vicious cycle.

After the third treatment her beautiful dark brown hair started to fall out by the handful. Without question, this was completely devastating for her. Within two weeks she was almost completely bald and a wig was in order, a gift from her sister Roberta. Anne would divulge later that this was the beginning of the end of her dignity.

The worst part of our trips to the clinic would be the long waits for treatment, sometimes upward of four hours. I could not help but marvel at the level of patience displayed by those waiting along with us. Most had come to terms with their cancer and you could sense a quiet resolve. Competent, sensitive and friendly clinic staff members also contributed to an overall relaxed atmosphere in the clinic and helped make a stressful experience at least tolerable.

Most days the waiting room was filled to overflowing—children, teenagers, adults of all ages, people in wheelchairs, people on oxygen ventilators—all bravely hoping for the best. We would get to know some of the regulars on a first name basis and then after a while we would not see them again. We couldn't help but wonder . . .

A MYSTERY PARALYSIS, JUST TO COMPLICATE MATTERS

Several days after her fourth chemo treatment Anne experienced a strange paralysis on the right side of her face, affecting her ability to speak and eventually working its way down to her shoulder, arm and hand. We were at a loss to know what to do, but after about 10 minutes the "freeze up", as she called it, stopped as suddenly as it had begun. Over the course of the next 48 hours she would have 10 similar attacks of the paralysis on the right side of her body.
Needless to say, her oncologist was consulted but he was unable to offer an explanation for the unusual attacks, except to say that he was convinced that they were not as a result of the chemotherapy. He immediately ordered x-rays, ultrasound and a spinal tap and arranged for Anne to see a neurologist.

The neurologist was equally puzzled and and promptly arranged for an MRI scan at Toronto General Hospital. The paralyzing attacks continued and chemotherapy treatment was suspended pending reports on the various tests and examinations. We were on pins and needles.

After two unsettled weeks the unexplained hit-and-run paralysis began to subside. Coincidentally, and much to his credit, a conscientious x-ray technician at Peel Memorial remembered an article he had seen in a medical journal reporting on a case in the U.S. similar to Anne's. He contacted the American doctor and obtained further information. A re-examination of Anne's x-rays revealed a culprit blood clot in the front portion of her brain.

Much to our relief, follow up x-rays revealed that the blood clot had dissipated and we were told that chances of it ever happening again were extremely remote. Anne waited another three weeks before she was physically and mentally ready to resume chemotherapy. It took most of 1992 for her to start feeling reasonably well again, but she was never able to return to work and was declared permanently disabled. Little by little she was able to do some light housekeeping and eventually join friends for lunch outings and shopping. Her tumor even appeared to have shrunk a bit. In spite of everything, we had a lot for which to be thankful.

Her smile and appearance were "deceiving" While she feared death, Anne became an advocate of the power of positive thinking. She shrugged off sympathy and patronization. She had a cheerful word for everyone, which was more often than not a cover for how sick she really was. People would remark on how good she looked, to which she would laughingly respond: "Well, looks can be deceiving." On checkup visits, her doctors would marvel at how well she had done. "We don't know what you're doing, but just keep doing it," they would say. She was dubbed "the miracle lady".

Out of necessity we adjusted our lifestyle considerably and established certain priorities. I began taking on part-time freelance work that enabled me to spend more time at home with Anne. Little by little, I became chief cook and bottle washer. The role of primary caregiver was soon to follow. In some convoluted way, the hiatus enabled us to divert attention to our oldest daughter, Debbie, who was diagnosed with cancer of the cervix, just a year after giving birth to her second child. Debbie underwent a radical hysterectomy and after an anxious few months her recovery was uncomplicated and complete.

We began to notice disturbing changes in Anne's tumor in the spring of 1995 and it became necessary for us to apply bandages in order to contain drainage. Her breathing was heavy again and she had to rely more and more on her "puffers". Fatigue set in once more and some days she just stayed in bed around the clock.

As if it wasn't enough that we had Anne's deteriorating condition to worry about, my 92-year-old mother's health was also rapidly failing and it became necessary for her to be moved into a nursing home. I felt as though I was the rope in a tug of war that no one could win. Four months after entering the nursing home and five days after stubbornly insisting that she be returned to her home in Dresden, my mother passed away. As an only child and sole survivor, it fell on me to settle affairs of the estate and to sell the family home, leaving Anne behind in Brampton for several hours or a day at a time. I couldn't go through that again for love nor money.

Funny, isn't it, how just when you think things can't get any worse, they always seem to? But on the other hand, we all have a reserve of strength that we can call on in times of difficulty. If we hold on to our spirituality we can rise to any occasion. That is the miracle of humankind.

Following a heart-to-heart talk with her oncologist, and convinced that there was no other course open to her, Anne hesitantly agreed to another eight rounds of chemotherapy. She was told that this would be a new form of chemo with few side affects. What really turned the trick for her was the oncologist's assurance that she would not lose her hair again. Well, famous last words! . . . Her hair began falling out after the second treatment and the wig that she hoped to never see again was resurrected. Losing a head of hair, not once but twice in a four-year period, was a cruel twist of fate.

Her reaction to the new chemo was more severe than before. Once tipping the scales at a "pleasing" 160, her weight plummeted to 90 pounds. The chemo was doing to her what up to then the cancer had been unable to do—kill her. After the fifth treatment the oncologist agreed that she might not survive a sixth. "We just can't do this to you any more," he sighed. Community Care services helped greatly

To complicate matters even further, the tumor was now the size of a football and subject to massive hemorrhaging. Her breathing became so labored that fluid had to be removed from her lungs, by no means a pleasant procedure. Through the Community Care Access Centre of Peel we were granted daily home care nursing assistance. Many of Anne's extremely expensive drugs and all tumor dressing materials were also provided under the program, affording us a quality of care that would otherwise have been beyond the reach of our fast-dwindling resources. Similarly, she was tested and qualified for a Canada Department of Health program that provided a crucial in-home oxygen service.

By now, Anne was spending much of her time in bed and because of the tumor bleeding problem and other personal needs, she could no longer be left alone. I had no choice but to phase myself out of a number of personal involvements and to completely stop working so that I could devote myself fully to the role of caregiver. We could not afford to lose my income but sometimes in life you have to make trade offs. If only Revenue Canada would recognize the financial implications of such trade offs, but that's another story.

Meal preparation, house cleaning, laundry and grocery shopping were easy chores compared to the cram course I had to take in learning about catheters and bed pans, patient hygiene, equipment sterilization, changing a bed with a person still in it, oxygen management, duragesic patch application, tumor dressings and, most importantly, how to stay calm in an emergency situation.

Initially I wanted to do everything for Anne myself and looked on any offer of assistance as an encroachment on our life and my responsibility. I was told that this is a natural reaction for most care givers in the early stages. I changed my do-it-all attitude, however, when I realized that if I wore myself out we most assuredly would both go down the tubes. They don't have courses in care giving for husbands who suddenly find themselves in such unfamiliar territory. Perhaps they should.

We managed to get through Christmas "97 and New Year's Day, but she was so uncomfortable that it became obvious to both of us that hospital care was again immanent. The first night back in hospital Anne was hooked up to a morphine drip without verification as to what her tolerance level might be or what other pain killer drugs she had been taking. She spent the next 48 hours totally out of it and as a precautionary measure was moved to palliative care where she was under 24-hour watch. We almost lost her because of that oversight but I chose not to press the issue with hospital authorities. I just wanted Anne to get better.

It was ironic that at home Anne had carefully monitored her medication, making a written note of every pill and the time she had taken it. She arrived at a very fine line, choosing to put up with more pain than the average person so that she could keep a clear mind and remain in control of her faculties. She hated the "spaced out" feeling.

It took the better part of a week for her to stabilize. After a series of tests it was decided that her tumor should be given priority. Thus began a two-week endurance test of 10 daily ambulance trips to the Ontario Cancer Centre at Sunnybrook Hospital in Toronto for palliative radiation treatments.

Believe it or not, Anne shared one ambulance trip with a second patient who had been picked up at a private residence and was destined for another hospital in Toronto. Much to our horror, we learned the next day that the other party was a carrier of the highly contagious and deadly MRSA bacteria (Methicllin Resistant Staphylococcus Aureus). Anne was immediately quarantined for 48 hours and subjected to a series of precautionary tests which, luckily for all concerned, came back negative. Given Anne's rock bottom immune system, this was just another in a long list of minor miracles for her.

Surprisingly and miraculously, Anne suffered no ill effects from the exhausting two-week ordeal, other than a sore throat from the carefully aimed radiation target so dangerously close to vital organs. She improved enough over the course of the next month that she could return home once again. I hurriedly arranged for a special bed for her and converted our dining room into a glorified hospital room, complete with all her familiar things including family photographs, privacy curtains, a television and comfortable chairs for visitors. The contents of a china cabinet were removed and replaced with medical supplies.

Unfortunately, on her fifth night at home she attempted to make her way to the bathroom alone in the dark. She somehow got tangled up in her oxygen tubing and fell, twisting her already weakened spine. Luckily, she did not break any bones but, sadly, she would never walk again.

Several days later she experienced excruciating stomach pain and was rushed to Mississauga Hospital as a redirect patient. After a series of tests and injections the hospital's head surgeon was sitting in front of us explaining that x-rays had shown air in Anne's bowel, probably the result of a perforation caused by the assortment of heavy cancer related drugs she had been given in the previous five or six years.

"There are rare cases such as yours where symptoms for an ulcer don't show up until it perforates, penetrating the wall or membrane of the stomach. It's a life-threatening situation, one that generally requires immediate surgery and a colostomy." he explained matter-of-factly. "With your cancer and weakened condition, however, you would never survive the surgery and I'd advise against it. We'll put you on a strong dose of antibiotics to slow down the poison that will gradually spread through your system, but you can expect the worst in about 72 hours. So if you have arrangements to make . . ."

"Am I hearing correctly?" I asked, to which Anne added: "Are you saying that I'm going to die?"

The words "yes, I'm afraid so" still ring in my ears. While Anne accepted her death forecast with relative resignation, I went into a state of shock and premature grief that lasted for days. I resolved to remain at her side in hospital to the bitter end.

In a telephone conversation with our family doctor the next morning, he expressed dismay over what had happened. " . . . But think of it this way, Dick, the poor dear girl has suffered more than enough. This may well be an out for her. Hang tough!"

To make my extended stay as comfortable as possible, a very attentive nurse provided me with a pillow, extra sheets and a pad for the recliner chair in Anne's room that would be my bed for the next 28 days. Our assigned doctor was extremely caring and interested in Anne's case, visiting her daily and making sure she was properly attended to as the anitibiotics and increased dosage of morphine took effect. She would slip in and out of consciousness with periods of delirium, but generally she was responsive and knew what was happening. She defied the odds once again.

At approximately the 60-hour mark, with our two daughters at her side, I thought Anne might be slipping away and each one of us, in our own way, said our goodbyes. Suddenly, however, I detected a change in her breathing and her body seemed to relax. She squeezed my hand and reached out to the two girls on either side of her, saying in a weak voice: "It's okay."

A glimmer of hope. Another miracle in the making? Seventy-two hours came and went. Then another 48 hours and Anne seemed to be slightly improved—stronger, more alert. "Well, since you're still here, maybe we should take some more x-rays and see what's happening," the doctor said as he shook his head in wonder.

The smile on his face as he entered the room the next afternoon spoke volumes. "It's nothing short of a miracle," were the first words out of his mouth. "The x-rays are clear, showing that there has been a spontaneous healing of the perforation. It's virtually unheard of, but the antibiotics obviously did their job. You are really one strong lady," he added.

He went on to say that they did find a small ulcer near the bend in her stomach and that he would be prescribing medication that she probably would have to take for the rest of her life. "Otherwise, we'll just start working on getting you strong enough so that you can go home again in a couple of weeks. I'm just so happy for you."

The depths of grief and despair one minute and sheer euphoria the next. I hardly knew how to react. I remember uttering a "thank you", but beyond that I was rendered speechless. Anne's reaction was typically off-handed: "I knew all along that I wasn't going to die." She was no doubt telling the truth, but why did she keep us guessing for so long?

Somehow, several nurses found out that Anne's birthday was February 28 and that mine was the next day (March 1). All the night nurses in palliative care got together and brought us a cake, complete with candles, and sang happy birthday. They knew that we were celebrating more than just our birthdays and it was their way of sharing their feelings with us. I hope they understood how much we appreciated their thoughtfulness.

On the 26th day of her stay, it was suggested that there was nothing more that could be done for Anne in hospital and she could be released the following day if she felt comfortable with the idea. A palliative care patient in two different hospitals in a three-month period and she was still alive to talk about it? Unheard of . . . Once again Anne had beaten the odds. The health care system worked for us.

When I think about our exposure to five different hospitals during our journey, it all seems like an unbelieveable dream. We experienced the good and the bad in our over-extended health care system, but on balance there were more pluses than minuses and we were thankful for that. Maybe we were lucky. And when today I hear about lengthy waiting periods for MRIs and radiation, and patients travelling to various parts of the province and into the U.S. for treatment, I have nothing but sympathy.

Realistically, too, it is not a perfect world and there are limits to the health care services our tax dollars can provide. The Canada Health Act aside, we have to take responsibility for our own health and that of our loved ones. Ultimately, when illness comes, it behooves us to be prepared to be flexible in our attitude and expectations, knowing that life is only as good as we make it.

Unbelievable as it may seem, Anne survived another three years of her physical and emotional roller coaster ride. Totally invalided and with the creepy crawly cancer working its way through her body, she would have two good days and then two bad ones. Sometimes we laughed and sometimes we would cry. Sometimes we would disagree and then we would agree. Sometimes we would agree to disagree. Sometimes we felt like giving up, then we would try all the harder to carry on.

We were so engrossed in today that we would forget about yesterday. We faced tomorrow when it came. We marvelled at each new sunrise and we embraced the day.

The thread of living one day at a time is woven throughout the fabric of the ages. It is a lesson we all learn with difficulty, but it is one that held the key to a peaceful existance for the Wrights as they faced an uncertain future. We came to the understanding that we were unduely hard on ourselves when we attempted to bear tomorrow's burdens with today's strength.

In quiet moments I studied Anne as she slept with life-sustaining oxygen tubes hissing up her nostrels. I often wished that I could crawl into her frail head to find out what it was really like to just lay there, day in and day out, totally dependent on others for every need—what it was really like to have accepted the fact that right now is about as good as it is ever going to get. More than once she opened her eyes and caught me watching her, prompting a groggy scolding: "Don't you know you can wake a person up by staring at them?" She always had a knack for disarming me. I would later test her theory one more time but, sadly, it didn't work.

While she fought against constant stomach and bowel distress and the tumor which had gradually spread across her entire chest and started to hemmorhage again (blood sometimes spurting to the ceiling and requiring me to apply finger tip pressure to the wound opening for upward of an hour), Anne continued to be an astute manager of her pain, preferring to stay with two Duragesic (fentanyl) 100 mcg/h patches supplemented sparingly with Statex (morphine sulfate) for breakthrough relief. To stay as alert as possible through the day, she resisted other sedatives until ready to settle down for the night. Her blood count dipped to dangerously low levels and she received transfusions on two occasions.

She was the only person I know who when asked if she was feeling pain would say "yes, but it is a good pain because it lets me know that I am still alive."

"I don't know why I'm still here," she would often add, "God must have a reason."

One thing for certain, we would not have made it as far as we did without the prayers and support of family and friends. We were also the benefactors of a wonderful home care network that inluded nurses who tended to Anne for an hour each day, a doctor who visited periodically and volunteers who sat with Anne while I looked after grocery shopping and other necessary chores outside the home. Our two daughters, a number of close friends and a sister and father in London, were just a phone call away whenever we needed them.

There was comfort and security for Anne in the warmth and tranquility of our home. From her bed in our former dining room, she had her finger on the pulse of the household. She scrutinized just about every move I made, particularly in the kitchen. While our roles were somewhat reversed, I needed no reminder of who was still "the boss".

Joy came in the form of grandchildren, three of which Anne originally thought she would never see. She enjoyed visitors but as time wore on she was reluctant to have anyone see her. "I just look so terrible and it takes so much out of me trying to have a conversation," she would explain. "I'm tired of living and I'm tired of dying."
I knew exactly what she meant.

We were both paying a toll. I began to experience varying degrees of melancholy. I would cry at sad things and it would be the same with happy things—music, children, acts of kindness, you name it and I would well up. On several occasions I broke down, collapsing to the floor and weeping uncontrolably for extended periods. Our doctor perscribed the anti-depressant Celexa and it helped in leveling out my emotions. It still does.

I do not recall Anne crying even once in the last year of her life. I can't help but think that she needed a different form of release—a more permanent one. Previously a sensitive, feeling person, it was almost as if she did not want to waste her precious time and energy on trivial earthly matters and just closed her mind to most of it. At one point she did hint that she could not allow herself to cry because it just took too much out of her and if she ever started she would never stop. That, in my book, is what you call control. Typically Anne.

We purposely did not make long-range plans toward the end, but we marked one date on the calendar, July 16, the day we would celebrate our 40th wedding anniversary. Anne and I made a wager. I bet that she would make it through to the 16th and beyond. She bet that she would not.

Unable to hang on any longer, Anne slipped away quietly and mercifully on the evening of July 6th., and won the bet by a mere 10 days.

I don't remember if we actually put a dollar amount on our wager. It was a life—or-death kind of thing and I guess I'll always be indebted to her, never knowing how much I owe.

FOOTNOTE:

Someone once said that avoiding the hurt of losing a loved one is like denying the disconfort of a sprained ankle. Not caring for the inury can result in further physical damage.

We tend to avoid the sting of reality with positives like "God doesn't give you more than you can bear" . . ."She is in heaven now" . . ."They'd want you to be strong, not cry" . . ."Think of the good things about their life."

By all means believe in heaven, believe in the best of life, believe that you will find strength in overcoming tragedy; but above all, grieve first. Give yourself permission to let it out, let it happen. Try to maintain your ability to laugh as well as cry, and mix in a good dose of patience and self-care.

Trust me, it does get better. It is difficult to put into words, but eventually you will become more at peace with your loss. There will always be pangs of sadness, but you move on.

And another thing, if there is someone in your life at present who you love dearly, put down this book and go tell them how you feel. Do it now! You might not get another chance.

Sincere graditude to Rosanne for her love, support and understanding as I worked my way through this project.

DICK WRIGHT

CHAPTER 10

A MESSAGE FROM HEAVEN

O N THE EVE of the funeral of my wife Anne, grandson Joshua (then five years of age) asked his mother Cindy if there was any way he could "talk" to his grandmother in Heaven. Thinking quickly, his mother confirmed that communicating with his grandmother would be possible. All he had to do was talk to her just as he had when she was alive. "In this way you can send messages back and forth to Gramma in Heaven," she explained.

> There was a brief pause and then: "Oh, wait," exclaimed Joshie, "I'm getting a message now."

> "From Gramma?" Cindy asked.

> "Yes!" Joshie replied.

> "What is she saying," was the natural next question from Cindy.

> With eyes glancing upward, the five-year-old responded without hesitation: "She says, 'I love you too'!"

Taken by surprise, Cindy discreetly chose not to push further. She would later divulge that at the time she was attempting to comfort her son during a very confusing and sad period in their lives but, instead, it was Joshie's words that gave her comfort. Out of the mouths of babes . . . !

There is nothing I can add to this story. It is what it is. I resist rationalization and speculation. But just think for a moment: " . . . love you too!"

Gramma's "message" was the thing.

CHAPTER 11

IMMORTALITY IN OUR LIVES

I WANT TO play devil's advocate on the subject of everlasting spirit for just a moment.

If we truly perish with the body and there is no such thing as immortality, then our whole system of laws, manners and usages on which society is founded, is nothing more than an impostor. The maxims of charity, patience, justice, honor, gratitude and friendship, which sages have taught over the centuries and which we ourselves practice, would be nothing but empty words possessing no real and binding efficacy. Why then would we heed them?

And if we were to dismiss the notion of eternal life, what would become of tender family ties wife, husband, parent, sister, brother or friend? How absurd it would be to honor that which has no existence. How frivolous it would be to concern ourselves for those whose end, like our own, must soon be annihilation.

In truth, however, if we were to accept the sway of reason eternally espoused by nonbelievers the whole world, as we know it, would fall back into a frightful chaos:

    —all the relations of life would be confounded;

    —all the ideas of vice and virtue would reverse;

    —the most inviolable laws of society would vanish;

    —all moral discipline would perish;

—the government of nations would no longer have the cement to hold them together;

—harmony of the body politic would become discord;

—the human race would be no more than an assemblage of barbarians.

Such would be the world if belief In God and immortality were to die out of the human heart.

The external life of mankind is the creature of time and circumstance, and passes away, but the internal abides and continues to exist. Spirit triumphs over form. That is the basis of everything we hold sacred and everything that makes the world what it is today.

CHAPTER 12

LIFE AFTER DEATH

T HOUGHTS FOR THIS item were formed some time ago and tucked away in the back of my mind during a protracted death bed vigil for a loved one. I really do not know why the thoughts are surfacing now, but I have a gut feeling that they might be relevant to someone, somewhere, at this time.

I once read that we are all infected with a sexually transmitted disease which is 100 per cent fatal. It is called "life". You can twist it, or deny it, but there is no escape. I thought at first that this was a rather unusual analogy, but after I considered the words a little more carefully I fully understood.

The question remains however, is there an end when death occurs? Or, is it the beginning of a new stage of our evolution? This is a subject about which countless writers have written, poets have sung, philosophers have speculated, and law makers have legislated. We come without knowing why, we go without knowing why, and in the words of Arthur Brisbane, "we travel our journey balanced on a thread stretched between the finger and thumb of destiny."

Dr. Carl Jung, the famous Viennese psychoanalyst, seemed to support Biblical references to a "life hereafter" when he wrote: "What happens after death is so unspeakably glorious that our imagination and our feelings do not suffice to form even an approximate conception of it." I tend to accept what he was saying. Just think of an amazing, limitless future where sorrow, imperfection, pain and mental and physical limitations will be no more. It's exciting, but difficult to comprehend, isn't it? This is where we call on faith and trust for comfort and hope.

The teachings of all faiths on what lies ahead of our present life span, and in the case of Christians, the solidity of a belief in a "bodily" resurrection (a spiritual body, not a physical one) makes all the difference between being able to keep going on with renewed energy, hopefulness and purpose, and being completely overcome by depression and despair. We feel sad and we naturally mourn the death of a loved one, but in the end we can celebrate their passing into a better realm, or stage the same one that we ourselves will experience some day, providing we have lived a decent kind of life. This is all a sound basis for ultimate hope for ourselves, our loved ones and the rest of humanity. It is what, in essence, keeps us on a relatively straight and narrow path during our earthly journey.

Death then, is not to be feared. It is to be welcomed and prepared for. What lies beyond death should be considered a reward for doing our best in the time allotted us on this earth, doing good more times than we did bad, receiving and extending forgiveness, loving unconditionally. Death, as I have witnessed it, is a quiet, peaceful release. We, the living, are left behind for the time being to complete our journey, advisedly maximizing every minute, every mile. Our dear departed loved ones would have it no other way.

CHAPTER 13

THE DIRECTION OF OLIVE'S LIFE

F ROM TIME TO time I am moved to write about individuals who
   have impressed me as I've journeyed life's pathway. For no particular
reason other than the fact that the following is a story that deserves to be
told, this is one of those times.

Most Canadians who were witness to the Diefenbaker era in Canadian politics
will share a tableau of Rt. Hon. John and Olive Diefenbaker, inseparable.
Wherever Mr. Diefenbaker's lengthy political life (Prime Minister 1957-'63)
and duties took him, Mrs. Diefenbaker was usually alongside.

No outsider can put into adequate words the deep bonds of affection and
understanding that make a close marital relationship. The strength of the
Diefenbaker's marriage was evident, however, in their public life together.
There remains a lasting image of Olive on public platforms, travelling,
mingling with crowds, always self-composed, an unobtrusive influence,
her presence and personal warmth an obvious source of pride and support
for her husband. Theirs was a touching public companionship. "Dief the
Chief", as he was affectionately called, could certainly be difficult and testy
at times, but in Olive's presence he was as soft as warm butter.

"The whole direction of my life is that I am John's wife," Mrs. Diefenbaker
said in an interview in 1975. She attributed the strength of their relationship
partly to the fact that they married in maturity, both in their 50s as widow
and widower. In total they had 23 years together.

Then Managing Editor of The Herald in Prince Albert, Saskatchewan (Dief's
home riding), I undertook a special edition of the newspaper honoring
the former prime minister on his 80th birthday, September 18, 1975. In
conjunction with the tribute edition, I was granted a rare interview with

Mrs. Diefenbaker that resulted in one of my longest conversations with her—but virtually no story.

I envisioned a feature piece based on Olive's impressions and opinions. The "My Life With John Diefenbaker as told by Oliver Diefenbaker" theme, I thought, would be a natural. We talked openly and casually for the better part of 90 minutes and she volunteered for the first time several personal details that would have been journalistic scoops in the day and fodder for some stimulating reading.

As the interview drew to a close, however, she interjected in her quiet, yet persuasive manner: "Of course, you will not be printing any of this, will you?" Talk about a letdown. I hardly knew how to respond.

She went on to explain that it was her policy to stay in the background and never become involved in publicity of any kind. "The minute he (John) became prime minister in 1957 I never opened my peeper again," she said convincingly. "I would prefer that if you write anything, that you put into your own words the love that John has for his fellow man. That's it—love, and they love him too! He has done so much for people. No one will ever know how much. I hope you understand," she added.

I was trying very hard to understand, and at least I felt honored that she confided in me as much as she did. At that point I did not have the heart to negotiate with her. I later tore up my notes and manufactured a rather nebulous piece for the special edition which, I was told later, met with the Diefenbakers' approval. In fact, Dief was "deeply touched" by the edition as a whole. Needless to say he held nothing back when it came time for his interview.

Olive suffered the first in a series of strokes several months later and Mr. Diefenbaker had tears in his eyes as he sat in my office at The Herald and sadly reported: "My dear wife is slipping badly but she remains in good spirits. She puts up a good front for my sake, I know. She is just an amazing woman."

As Olive was forced to share John will all of Canada, he shared her with his "fellow Canadians". Throughout the last year of her life, in and out of hospital, Mrs. Diefenbaker received a steady flow of mail from people across Canada expressing concern and affection. Until shortly before her last illness, she was still handwriting replies to her mail at a daily rate that reached in excess of 50 personal messages.

John did not last long after Olive passed away. His heart was broken and I know he could not live without her.

She may never have "opened her peeper", but many aging Canadians like me remember the charm that warmed hundreds of encounters on the political campaign trail and countless social functions across the country. Olive Diefenbaker was always there, at John's side. Attentive, serene.

CHAPTER 14

THE CHURCH LADIES

I HAVE FOND memories of my early exposure to the wonderful work of "women of the church". Regardless of denomination, the faithfulness and commitment of women's organizations have, without question, been the life blood of all churches.

At a very early age I came to realize what "women of the church "really stood for, be they auxiliaries, societies, ladies aid, missionary groups whatever. I remember very clearly being relegated to my upstairs bedroom on the evenings when my mother hosted church group meetings. I would curl up on the floor with my ear cupped to the grate that allowed warm air from downstairs to circulate to the upper floor level. I would listen to what was transpiring in the parlour and living room below—the prayers, the hymns, the committee reports, the updates on care packages and thos coarse khaki wool socks and mitts lovingly knit by the ladies for the troops, "our boys", overseas. Of course there would always be at least one fund-raising program on the agenda to help bolster church coffers.

I was able to put a face to every voice that came up through the grate and I was fascinated by what was being said and who was saying it:

A school teacher, the banker's wife, a public health nurse, my Aunt Hattie, my best friend's mother, a farm lady who delivered eggs to us every Thursday, our choir leader with her unmistakable laugh, the minister's wife with her quiet voice of reason, occasionally my mother the collective face and voice of mission and outreach in churches, small and large, around the globe to this day.

Looking back now, maybe I was hard pressed for entertainment. Maybe I was just curious. Remember that there were no televisions, computers or cell phones in kids' bedrooms in those days. Certainly, it was a different era and I am glad that I was exposed to it. At that impressionable age I came to understand how the efforts of a small group of women could reach around the world.

I would generally drift off to sleep just as tea cups began to tinkle amidst the hum of female conversation at the conclusion of the business portion of the meetings. All was right with my world. I could depend that there would be leftover peanut butter cookies and at least one date square put aside for me next day . . . Mrs. McFadden would see to it. I was warm, I was secure, God was in Heaven and "The Church Ladies" had everything under control.

Fond memories all, and an appreciation for the work that church women have continued over the decades with much dedication and little fanfare. I dare say that there are no inquisitive little boys eavesdropping on meetings these days, but it goes without saying that God has an ear to His Heavenly "grate" and He blesses all church women for what He hears.

DICK WRIGHT

CHAPTER 15

CAPITAL FOR A LIFETIME

C HARACTER, AS DEFINED in Webster's New World Dictionary: "a distinctive trait, quality or attribute; an individual's pattern of behavior or personality; moral constitution; moral strength; self-discipline, fortitude; reputation."

If I were asked today what is the most important investment that a young person can make as they enter adulthood and venture into the real world of making a living, I would have to say that character is capital that should be established early and invested in often. Character, regarded as capital, brings a much surer yield of returns than any other form of investment in life. It is unaffected by panics and failures, fruitful when all other investments lie dormant and has as much promise in the present life as in that which is to come.

Benjamin Franklin attributed his success in the public eye, not to his talents or his communications skills, but to his known integrity of character. "Hence, it was," he said, "that I had so much weight with my fellow citizens. I was but a bad speaker, never eloquent, subject to much hesitation in my choice of words, hardly correct in language, and yet I generally carried my point." There is no disputing that character creates confidence in every station of life and Franklin was a good example of that.

The higher walks of life are treacherous and dangerous; the lower ever full of obstacles and impediments. We can only be secure in either, by maintaining those principles which are just, praiseworthy and pure, and which inspire bravery in ourselves and confidence in others. When Stephen of Coloma fell into the hands of his base assailants, and they asked him, in derision, "Where is now your Fortress?" He boldly replied "here", placing his hand over his heart.

Strength of character, then, consists of two things, power of will and power of self-restraint requiring for existence strong feelings and a strong command over them. Someone once said that deportment, honesty and a desire to do right carried out in practice, are to human character what truth, reverence and love are to religion, and I believe that to be true.

Oh sure, there are bound to be detractors and those who scoff at one's high standards of character, but it is not as much in their affected revulsion as it is in their wish to reduce them to the standards of their own degraded natures and vitiated passions.

That character is power is true in a much higher sense than the contention that knowledge is power. Mind without heart, intelligence without conduct, cleverness without goodness, are powers in one sense, but they are detrimental powers that lead without exception to failure and undoing.

Yes indeed, young people, investing early and often in your character as defined in the dictionary, is not only wise but essential. It is capital that costs nothing to accumulate. It pays huge dividends throughout your life . . . And you can take it with you when you go.

Hold fast to your capital, your investments in character and principles. The biggest mistake anyone could make would be to compromise their capital by cashing in even a small portion of it. The long-term cost implications are just too great.

DICK WRIGHT

CHAPTER 16

MOTHER: THE HOME
WE COME FROM

I THINK THAT there is general agreement that unconditional love of the parent corresponds to one of the deepest longings, not only of the child, but of every human being. It is little wonder that we all cling to the longing for the first love we experience in life—that of motherly love.

Mother is the home we come from, and this is not to diminish the role that fathers play in our lives. Fathers truly enter the picture after natural mother nurturing has taken place. They represent the other pole of human existence; the world of thought, of man-made things, of law and order, of discipline, of travel and adventure. Fathers show the child the road into the world and I talk more about this in the next chapter.

This piece is about mothers, however, and the best place to start is at the beginning.

Motherly love, as Enrich Fromm points out in The Art of Loving is unconditional affirmation of the child's life and needs. This affirmation has two aspects; one is the care and responsibility absolutely necessary for the preservation of the child's life and its growth. The other aspect goes further in that it is the attitude which instills in the child a love for living and enables feeling—it is good to be alive, it is good to be a little boy or girl, it is good to be on this earth.

It is interesting to note that these two aspects of motherly love are expressed very succinctly in the Biblical story of creation. God creates the world and man which corresponds to the simple care and affirmation of existence. On each day after creating nature and man, God says: "It is good." The same idea may be taken to be expressed in another Biblical symbolism.

The promised land (land is always a mother symbol) is described as "flowing with milk and honey." Milk is the symbol of the first aspect of love, that of care and affirmation. Honey symbolizes the sweetness of life, the love for it and the happiness of being alive. Most mothers are capable of giving "milk" but fewer are capable of giving "honey" too. By means of explanation, in order to give "honey", a mother must not only be a good mother, but happy in other areas of her life as well. A mother's love for life, her positiveness and cheerfulness, her love of others, is as infectious as is her anxiety. Both attitudes have a deep effect on the child's entire personality.

Certainly, one can distinguish among children—and adults—those who were given only "milk" and those who were blessed with both "milk and honey."

Unlike brotherly love and erotic love between equals, the relationship of mother and child is by its very nature one of inequality, where one needs all the help and the other gives it. It is for this altruistic, unselfish character that motherly love has been considered the highest form of love, and the most sacred of all emotional bonds. The mother transcends herself in the infant, her love for it gives her life meaning and significance. It seems, however, that the real achievement of motherly love lies not in her love of the infant, but in her continuing love of the growing child.

And grow, the child must. It must emerge from the mother's womb, from her breast; it must eventually become a complete separate human being. The very essence of motherly love is to care for the child's growth and that means to want the child's separation from herself, as difficult as it may be. Unlike other forms of love where people who were separate become one, in motherly love two people who were one become separate. It is only at this stage that motherly love becomes such a daunting task, that it requires unselfishness, the ability to give everything and to want nothing but the happiness of the loved one.

Only the really loving woman, the woman who is happier in giving than in taking, who is firmly rooted in her own existance, can be a loving mother when the child is in the process of separation. Motherly love for the growing child, love which wants nothing for oneself, is perhaps the most difficult form of love to be achieved.

Motherly love is half instinctive and half very hard work. It involves a lot of giving and very little receiving. Of course you mothers already knew that, didn't you.

DICK WRIGHT

CHAPTER 17

FATHERS NEED HELP

I MAY BE generalizing and idealizing a little too much, but the way I see it is that mothers have the primary function of making a child secure in life through unconditional love while the father's role is that of a teacher preparing the child to cope with the society within which it was born.

A father's love should be guided by principles and expectations; it should be patient and tolerant, rather than threatening and authoritarian. It should give the growing child an increasing sense of competence and eventually permit the youngster to become its own authority and to dispense with that of the father. Eventually, the mature person comes to the point where he/she has become free of the outside mother and father figures and has built them up inside. In contrast to Freud's concept of the super-ego, however, the child has built them inside not by incorporating mother and father, but by building a motherly conscience on its own capacity for love and a fatherly conscience based on his reason and judgment. (You'll no doubt need to read the forgoing at least one more time to grasp the essence of it.)

This all sets the stage for me to go off at a personal tangent.

I think that there is general agreement that studies, magazines, books and TV documentaries have helped women meet the changing demands of motherhood in recent years. They have been instrumental in teaching techniques of child care and examining the needs of both children and mothers. They offer advice, sympathy, humor and counselling while providing challenge and inspiration for being a mother.

Now look at men's magazines for instance: sports, business, investment, seduction, hobbies—but nothing to help a man be a father to a son or daughter. Let's face it, being a father today is not easy and it does not always come naturally. The old techniques just no longer apply. Once upon a time, a son worked by his father's side, sharing the satisfactions and the frustrations, the successes and failures of the field, the barn, the shop or store.

What model does a father follow today? Some fathers still choose the army model, demanding discipline and obedience. Others choose to be pals, playing street hockey or swapping teeenage jokes, being just one of the guys. Still others do not involve themselves much one way or the other, leaving parenting pretty much to the mother. Then of course, there is the other side of the gender coin—daughters, bless their hearts. Confused by the complexity of fathering a daughter, many dad's simply choose to back off completely when their girls reach the teenage stage. More and more I think there is a genuine fear of vulnerability—of not understanding, of making a mistake.

So how does a father fulfil what is expected of him? Where does he turn when self help is needed and desired? It is not a laughing matter. I truly believe fathers need help today more than ever. Consider too, increasing cases of single parent families where mothers are required to take on the unnatural role of fathering as well.

It is time our society took fatherhood more seriously. Government, service clubs, churches, community and business organizations, the media, should all be discussing this subject with the goal of establishing educational programs for desperate fathers who want to do the right thing in raising their children.

It cannot be taken for granted that every father will turn out to be as lucky as me. In "growing up" with my children, I tried my best and they became wonderful adults in spite of me.

DICK WRIGHT

CHAPTER 18

EASY TO KISS, EASY TO FORGET

A LOT OF what I write is for the benefit of my grandchildren, four being teenagers. Of course, as unbelievable as it may seem, we all were teens at one time, struggling to find identity and a niche in life, living each new experience with unbridled intensity and emotion.

The setting for this story is Cocoa, Florida, where I attended a baseball rookie training camp in the early months of 1956. Talk about "wet behind the ears", I was all of that and more. It was difficult enough trying to make the grade in professional baseball at 18 years of age but I also had to hopelessly fall in love for the first time, just to complicate matters.

"The face of an angel," I gasped as my eyes fell on a breathtaking countenance engulfed by a sea of church choir members. The worship service on that Sunday morning at St. Andrew's Presbyterian Church in Cocoa was a blur. That face in the choir was my sole focus. I was feeling something strange in the pit of my stomach. My heart was pounding. An unusual pulsating flush came over me.

As I left the sanctuary following the service I was startled by a tap on the shoulder. My heart jumped into my throat as I turned to see that face on a tall and statuesque body, standing in front of me. "Hi, my name is Sylvia. I saw you in the congregation and I just wanted to welcome you. Are you a ball player?" We chatted at length, exchanging information about ourselves on the church steps that unforgettable Sunday morning in the warm Florida sun. For a kid from small town Dresden, Ontario, this was the stuff of which dreams are made.

I learned that Sylvia was also 18 years of age and soon to graduate from high school. She played clarinet in the school band. Her mother was director of the church choir and her father was Chief of the nearby Cape Canaveral

Police Force (later to become Cape Kennedy). I don't remember what I told Sylvia about myself, but I must have divulged the name of the lady who owned the home where I had been billeted. "I'd better get going. My mother has been waiting," exclaimed "that face" as we parted company. The four block walk that followed was as if I was floating on a cloud. My feet must have hit the sidewalk at some point, but it didn't feel like it.

Several hours later I was in the process of composing a letter to my mother when I heard the downstairs telephone ring. "Just one moment. I'll get him for you . . . Dick, it's a call for you!" came my landlady's voice from the foot of the stairs. "It's a girl," she said with a wide grin and a wink as she passed the receiver over to me.

To my disbelief it was Sylvia on the other end of the line, asking me if I had been to the ocean yet. I hadn't and she invited me to take a trip to the beach after baseball the next day—"if I liked to". Needless to say, I liked to and we did. She picked me up in her parents' black 1955 Mercury and if this was a dream I didn't want to wake up. We had a glorious few hours ocean side, capped by an invitation to be her escort for the Cocoa District High School's annual Valentine's Ball. Adding to the honor of it all was the fact that Sylvia just happened to be a prime candidate for Queen of the Ball. I was also flabbergasted to learn that her up-to-then boy friend, a school basketball and football star named Bob, was also a shoe-in for King of the Ball. Needless to say, news that the potential Queen of the Ball would be escorted by an out of town baseball player and not the King-in-waiting, caused quite a stir in the school community.

Sylvia arranged for us to accompany two other couples, one of which would provide a car. Good thing too because I not only did not have access to a vehicle, I did not yet even have a driver's licence. Sylvia met me at her front door on the evening of the grand occasion and introduced me to her parents as I presented her with a break-the-bank orchid corsage. Another more uncomfortable introduction awaited me an hour later in the school auditorium.

"Bob, I want you to meet Dick Wright," Sylvia enthused to the hulking six foot plus, 200 pound figure looming large in front of me. As we shook hands, I got the distinct impression that Bob was not all that impressed. I was certainly not one of his favorite people at that particular juncture in time and undoubtedly there was potential for someone else to be "crowned" that evening. I would have liked to know Bob better but something seemed to

DICK WRIGHT

tell me that it would be advisable for me to stay clear of him for the duration of my stay in Cocoa.

The evening was an unqualified success. As expected, Sylvia and Bob were crowned Queen and King and I was overcome with apprehension as the Ball drew to a close. That apprehension was altered somewhat when Sylvia gently rested her head on my shoulder on our way home and softly whispered: "I don't want us to kiss tonight. My mother kept saying over and over today 'easy to kiss, easy to forget' and I don't want you to ever forget me." On one hand I understood but on the other I was let down just a bit. I don't remember anything about the brief balance of the evening. The words "easy to kiss, easy to forget" resonated in my ears—still do to this day. When I got back to my rooming house that night I noticed a slight smudge of lipstick on the lapel of my suit coat, left there by Sylvia when he snuggled close to utter those six mood altering words. I wore the suit for several years after that but could never quite bring myself to have the coat dry cleaned.

Shortly thereafter I signed a contract and shipped out to join my new team in Georgia. My heart was broken and, love-sick puppy that I was, cried a lot for a few days. I was happy to have the opportunity to continue playing baseball in the states but I was reluctant to leave Sylvia and all that she had come to mean to me. I never told her, but I was truly in love for the first time. I never knew that love could hurt so much. "I'll come back some day," I tried to assure myself.

As it turned out I never again saw Sylvia. We exchanged letters for several months but eventually we stopped corresponding. I don't know why. Long distance relationships are sometimes like that, especially when you are young with so much more to experience.

Sylvia's mother was probably right about that damn "easy to kiss, easy to forget" expression. I'm sure she would be pleased to know that I never did get to kiss her daughter. Likewise, I never forgot the face that so captured my fancy all those years ago. I wonder if her daughter remembers the kid from Canada that she too never got to kiss!?

CHAPTER 19

HOME SWEET HOME

THINK ABOUT THIS for a minute.

Where do you look forward to going after a hard day's work? When you are not feeling well, where do you want to be most? After a trip or a long vacation, what looks good to you? What is your shelter on a stormy day? When you think about parents and childhood, what immediately comes to mind? Where do you retreat to find rest from the toils and annoyances of life? In all the world, where do you feel the most comfortable? If you are lucky, where does your sweetheart live?

The answer to all those questions, of course, is "HOME" with its oh-so-familiar cracks, creaks, dents and characteristics known only by you. Home is warm! Home is safe! Personally, home is my sanctuary in every aspect of my life. It is my favorite place!

Oh sure, I enjoy travelling and visiting new places but I do less and less of it as the years pass. In truth, I have everything I need at home. The lure of other places pales in comparison to my desire to be home. I am sure it is that way for most readers of Wrights Lane.

The word home touches every fibre of the soul and strikes every chord of the human heart. Nothing but death can break its spell. What tender associations are linked with home? What pleasing images and deep emotions it awakens. It calls up the fondest memories of life and opens in our nature the purest, deepest, richest gush of consecrated thought and feeling.

So many expressions have been coined around home.

-Home sweet home.—Home is where the heart is.—Home is where you hang your hat.—It takes a lot of livin' to make a house a home.—There's no place like home.

Essays, poems and songs have been written about home, the most popular being the 150-year-old song "Home! Sweet Home!"

"Mid pleasures and palaces though we roam, Be it ever so humble, there's no place like home."

Sung like a hymn but originally a secular song, Home! Sweet Home! is a story about somebody going away from home, roaming around, falling on hard times, and then going back home to get a soothing caress from mother and a fond smile and pat on the back from father.

None of us were yet around at the time, but history records that some 20,000 people gathered in old Castle Garden, New York, to hear Jennie Lind sing, as no other songstress ever had, the sublime compositions of Beethoven, Handel and other music masters. In the middle of her performance it seems that the Swedish Nightingale had a flash of nostalgia. She began to think of her home and paused briefly before pouring forth, with deep emotion, "Home! Sweet Home!"

The audience could not stand it. An uproar of applause stopped the music. Tears gushed from those thousands like rain. Beethoven and Handel were forgotten. After a long pause Jennie resumed the song, her voice seemingly coming from heaven, almost angelic. It was one of those special moments and it was the word "home" that bound, as with a spell, 20,000 souls that day.

When we look at the simplicity and brevity of "Home! Sweet Home!" we are moved to ask, what is the charm that lies concealed in this classic song? The answer is easy. Next to religion, the deepest and most endurable sentiment in the human soul is that of our feelings for home. Every heart vibrates to this theme.

Home has an influence which is stronger than death. It is law to our hearts, and binds us with a spell which neither time nor change can break.
For me, it is an inspiring hope that, when we separate from this earth, there is an eternal home awaiting us on the other side. Sweet home! Beautiful home! Glorious home! Peaceful home! Home with each other! Everlasting home!.

Through the grace of God, we will always have a place to call "home".

CHAPTER 20

LIFE GAME PLAN
GOOD STRATEGY

HERE I GO again "preaching" to young people. I promise that The Old Coach will give it a rest after making this one last point.

There are two paths in life and it is crucial for the young man or woman, emerging from the relative comfort of their carefree teens, to consider these two ways soberly and earnestly before moving on. If they choose a path that truth and reason tell them will lead to honor, success and happiness, they have chosen wisely. The other path is too well known to need description.

It is a sad awakening when, after a lapse of 20 years, we find ourselves amid ruined hopes—to sit down with folded hands and say, "So far I have failed. Life really sucks! Is this what I can expect for the rest of my life?" Trust me, I have been there, so naive that I actually thought that my dreams and fantasies alone were enough to carry me through. Only trouble was, I washed out as a student and I had no life game plan beyond baseball at which I was a has-been at 19-years-of-age. In the absence of a plan for my life, I really had to scramble to catch up. Sometimes I think that I am still playing catch up.

The first thing that I had to learn is that life is what you make it. If it is mean and cruel, it is because we make it so. The mystery of our being, the necessity of action, the relation of cause and effect, the dependence of one thing upon another, the mutual influence and affinity of all things, assure us that life is for a purpose and it can be quite fulfilling and wonderful.

Almost too late, I came to realize that at the outset of a career we must form the solemn purpose to make the most and the best of the powers—the strengths, the talents, the skills—that we were born with and to turn, to the best possible account, every outward advantage within reach. We are wise, also, to have a contingency or backup plan, should unforeseen circumstances develop in our life.

The purpose of which I speak should carry with it the assent of reason, the approval of conscience and the sober judgement of intellect. It should also embody within itself whatever is vehement in desire, inspiring in hope, thrilling in enthusiasm and intense in desperate resolve. Such a plan of life saves us from many a damaging contest or challenges that offer unhealthy temptations. It will regulate the way we approach our education, sports and recreational activities. For those just starting out in adulthood, I cannot emphasize enough the fact that by studying, training and laboring under the inspiration of such a purpose, there is every possibility of soaring out of sight of those who barely allow themselves to be carried along by the momentum of the machinery to which they are attached.

Many pass through life without even a consciousness of where they are, what they are, and what they are doing. They gaze on whatever lies directly before them in fond amusement lost. In effect, they never grow up!

I like the wisdom of the great football coach Vince Lombardi who said: "The quality of a man's (or woman's) life is in direct proportion to his (her) commitment to excellence, regardless of his (her) chosen field of endeavor."

And speaking of football, the NFL/NFF in the States has created a most commendable program as part of its youth development initiative. "Power 4W" consists of four important elements: Wishpower, Wantpower, Waypower and Willpower, all of which warrant closer scrutiny.

The first step, Wishpower, requires you to think about what you would like your life to be like in five or 10 years from now. Would you like to be in college, or if you are already would you like to be a doctor, business executive, actor or professional athlete? Would you like to have a family? This vision of the future must be your ideal, not what you would settle for. Don't be afraid to dream!

Having thought about the future, you need then to set the proper goals that will get you there. This is the step called Wantpower.

Goals are very important because they keep you motivated, give you direction, and give you a sense of pride and accomplishment once you achieve them.

Once you have set your goals, it is important to design a strategy or game plan in order to achieve them. In the Waypower stage it is helpful to complete a goal ladder which will allow you to climb toward you ultimate goal one step at a time and also make progress visible.

Of course, setting goals is much easier than actually achieving them. As I said previously, obstacles with potential to impede your progress, can arise at any time. If you are prepared with an effective defense and have the Willpower to overcome roadblocks, you will be on the way to an ideal future.

When problems arise, as they most assuredly will, take a deep breath, go for a walk, clear your mind so that you can put the situation in perspective. This will then allow you to think of all the choices that you have; which choices will lead you to the right decision and which options will lead to the wrong decision. Finally, respond to the situation with the decision that will get you one step closer to your goal—an ideal future for you and the special significant others who will come into your life.

Choose well, young people. We're pulling for you!

CHAPTER 21

ARE YOU IN HARMONY
OR HELLED?

"WITHIN YOURSELF LIES the cause of whatever enters into life. To come into the full realization of your own awakened interior powers, is to be able to condition your life in exact accord with what you would have it."—Ralph Waldo Trine, author, approx. 1896.

Optimists and pessimists are about as different as night and day. They are similar, however, in that each has a particular point of view that is a determining factor in their life. I have gone through most of my existence believing that it doesn't hurt to be a little pessimistic at times, providing of course that you are predominantly optimistic.

Truth be known: You can't be a little bit pessimistic any more than you can be a little bit pregnant. Optimism and pessimism are like oil and water, never blending no matter how hard you stir. I have been wrong in trying to mix the two and I don't mind admitting it.

I arrived at my current state of understanding by asking myself three questions. 1) Do I prefer strength or impotence? 2) Do I want peace or pain? 3) Do I aspire to success or failure? The answer in each case was obvious.

Optimists and pessimists both build their world from within based on perception. One, I believe, creates a type of heaven while the other contributes to a certain hell. You and I have the predominating characteristics of either an optimist or a pessimist. We are making, hour by hour, our own heaven or our own hell; and in the degree that we are making one or the other we are helping make it for all of mankind. There is very definitely a domino effect. In both cases we make a contribution to the world, one positive and one negative.

The optimist calls on wisdom and insight to maintain a positive attitude while the pessimist is questioning by nature and has a very narrow, limited view on life in general.

The word harmony has pleasing, heavenly connotations. The old English word hell means to build a wall around, to separate; to be helled was to be shut off from. If there is such a thing as harmony in our life there must be something that we are in sync with or in close relationship to. Likewise, if there is such a thing as being helled, then there must be something from which we are held or separated.

I always suspected that there was something holding me back for all these years and now I understand that it was ME keeping ME from being ME, aided and abetted by that little bit of pessimism that I thought was so healthy. I guess you are never too old to learn something about life—and yourself.

What all this means is that it is sometimes good to take a little personal inventory. The Greek philosopher Aristotle, a teacher of Alexander the Great and millions others more than 20 centuries ago, advocated just that. Be honest with youself. Ask the hard questions next time you are in a philosophical mood. And don't be pessimistic about the answers.

DICK WRIGHT

CHAPTER 22

OVERCOMING SHYNESS TAKES PRACTICE

I HAVE NOT done many things in life warranting an outward display of satisfaction and pride. But after some serious reflection and consideration, I can truly say that I am extremely proud of myself for overcoming a debilitating affliction—shyness. In fact, I have really come a long, long way. And you know what, it only took me about 65 years of conscious effort, and a lot of maturity to bring about this emotional change. Nature may have played a role too as it took its course through various awkward periods in my life.

I mention this now, particularly for the benefit of young people, because I know there is potential for shyness at a certain stage of personal development. I learned from firsthand experience that the danger of shyness is that it can often be mistaken for standoffishness or simply seen as unfriendliness, and this is indeed unfortunate. In my experience, shy people are very sensitive because of their listening skills and they are especially caring toward others.

An interesting Kidshealth article accurately describes shyness as "an emotion that affects how a person feels and behaves around others." Take it from me, shyness can mean feeling uncomfortable, self-conscious, nervous, bashful, timid or insecure. When a person feels shy, they might hesitate to say or do something because they feel unsure of themselves and they are not prepared to be noticed.

Experts have said that shyness is partly the result of genes and partly influenced by behaviors learned—the way people have reacted to their shyness and the experiences they have had in life. In my case, I think that I was born shy. When I was about four years of age, I used to play outside waiting for morning milk and bread deliveries. One day the milk man hesitatingly said to my mother as he made his weekly collection: "It's too bad about your son, Mrs. Wright!" Taken aback, my mother asked why he would say such a thing. "Well, isn't he deaf and dumb?" was the shocking response.

It seems the milk man would always stop to speak to me but I never answered . . . Never even gave indication that I had heard him. So he just assumed that I could neither hear nor speak.

As I grew older my shyness grew more painful. I would avoid eye contact, even pretend to not see people rather than have to speak to them. I felt bad about this. I wanted to be outgoing and friendly, but I just did not know how. Saying hello seemed excruciatingly difficult for me and I would even go so far as to practice saying things like "hello", "hi", "how are you?" with different expression and emphasis, but nothing seemed to come naturally.

There were times during social occasions when I would feel alone in a crowd. I would hesitate to try new things, preferring instead to watch others before joining in on a group activity. The world's greatest wall flower, it took me for ever to ask a girl to dance, even longer to go out on dates. My shyness, or backwardness, was so upsetting and frustrating for me as a teenager that many times I would just close myself in my bedroom and cry.

And on that note, a word of caution here for those who are close to a shy young person. If you push, tease or bully that person into a situation they are not prepared for, you can make them even more shy. Likewise, if parents are overly cautious or overprotective, it can teach the child to back away from situations that might be uncomfortable or unfamiliar. Understanding, love and support are what a shy youngster needs most. Confidence boosting and the occasional pat on the back will also work wonders.

In sports I was confident, aggressive and competitive but it took years for me to realize I could carry all of that into other areas of my life, if I wanted to.

One of the best things for me was getting a job in a retail store where I was forced to approach customers and to wait on them. Even then, for the better part of eight years, I died a thousand deaths with each customer that came in the store. Eventually, I became a newspaper reporter and there I was again having to take my communications to another level—digging for information, asking probing questions, gaining the confidence of others.

Strangely enough, I always enjoyed theatre and public speaking and through these interests I developed an ability to step outside of myself, to become someone else when I had to. The natural next step was to gain the internal confidence necessary to step out of my comfort zone when the opportunity presented itself. Like a lot of things in life, the more "stepping out" you do the more comfortable you become and before long you do not give it a second thought.

But as I have said before, I'm a slow learner. It took me until mid life to understand that practice truly does make perfect. Some of us, sad to say, have to practice social skills like assertiveness, conversation and friendly, confident body language, so that we can get the enjoyment from everyday experiences that we so longingly seek.

By the time I answered a call to take on church lay preaching assignments a few years ago, I did so with utmost confidence, free of self doubts and full of commitment. Stomach butterflies aside, I looked forward to each Sunday engagement and derived a great deal of satisfaction from the experience. So I am living proof that you can overcome shyness. It takes time, patience, courage and practice, but it is worth the hard work.

I am even going out of my way to talk to strangers now and if that isn't coming a long way, I don't know what is. Proud? Darn right I am!

The only pain I feel today is of a physical nature and I'm doing my best to deal with that too.

SHY GUY NOW TALKS TO STRANGERS

Sensitivity, sense of humor helpful

IN CASE YOU haven't already noticed, I'm an odd sort. I like to speak to perfect strangers—in stores, on the street, just about anywhere. What is so strange about this is the fact that I used to be extremely shy and reluctant to even acknowledge the presence of others, often looking the other way in order to avoid eye contact.

I really do not know how to explain the change in my personality other than the realization that as we mature we become more comfortable in our skin and we tend to open up and reach out more. I honestly feel that you do not have to know a person to speak to them as long as it is a light-hearted comment accompanied by a smile and a twinkle in the eye.

More often than not people react favorably to my unsolicited invasions. Surprise, at first, is generally followed by a smile and a few words of response. Of course I pick my targets carefully. I like to speak to young and old alike, people with frowns on their faces, people who appear to be deep in thought, people who are handicapped in some way. The payoff for me is to see someone relax, if only for a moment, and make the all-important person-to-person contact that is so lacking in many lives today. For instance, while in a cash-out line ahead of a First Nation couple, I happened to comment on the weather and made a reference to some high calorie food I had in my basket, adding: "Of course you folks are so slim and trim you don't have to worry about that." They laughed. When I left I heard the man say to the woman: "He was a nice guy, wasn't he!"

Of course reaction is not always favorable. The other day I was exiting Foodland grocery store with a cart full of groceries when a woman in her 50s came racing around the corner. Her body was going in one direction and her mind in another. I pulled my cart to a halt as she did a quick side step, narrowly avoiding a collision. "We've got to stop bumping into each other like this!" I laughingly commented. She stopped abruptly, removed her sun glasses and looked me square in the face for an uncomfortable few seconds. "I don't know you," she said as she turned on her heels and disappeared into the store.

A few days later I stopped off at Hi-Berry Farm to pick up a few items. I couldn't help but notice a middle aged couple painstakingly picking over a large counter of raspberries. It was my invitation to reach in front of them and randomly pick out a box of beautiful berries with a "there I think that I got the best one". Then it was over to the green beans a few minutes later and there they were again deliberating over each bean that they examined individually. As before, I reached in and scooped up a handful saying: "By golly, I think that I got the best ones again." The man (I think he may have been a retired farmer or police officer) turned and growled at me: "Are you just about through?" Some people just do not have a sense of humor.

It seems like I'm always buying food. I was at a diary case one day recently when I was joined by a neatly dressed older woman (she was older than me so that qualified as "old"). I could not help but detect a very pleasant aroma, prompting me to comment boldly: "You smell very nice today!" With a sweet smile she replied: "Thank you. It's Alfred Sung."

Sometimes responses are not only spontaneous but delivered with humor equal to mine. "How do you kiss your boy friend? I asked a young Kentucky Fried Chicken attendant sporting four protruding lip piercings. "Very carefully," was her surprise answer.

The one that really gave me cause to reconsider the consequences, however, involved a cute little girl and her mother. As they approached me on the sidewalk I noticed that the child was lagging behind her mother by quite a few yards. As little three and four year old girls do, she was pausing every few steps to adjust the dress on a doll she was carrying. As I passed her I said: "That is a very pretty dress on your doll." "Thank you," she said. "Her name is Cathy."

Continuing on my way, I heard the mother ask in a firm voice: "What did we say about talking to strangers?"

"He wasn't a stranger," the little one replied matter-of-factly.

CHAPTER 23

ONE GOOD NICKNAME
DESERVES ANOTHER

I SOMETIMES GET caught up in mind games that are a complete waste of time. Take today for instance. I've been running nicknames through my mind, prompted I guess by a recent obsession with my hometown of Dresden, the nickname capital of the world, where virtually everyone has a moniker of some sort. The more I thought about these stupid nicknames, the more I realized that many of them can be linked in an odd sort of way.

For instance, for every Bull there is a Moose, every Lefty has a Righty, every Skunk is Stinky and Nip and Tuck are tailored for each other. See what I mean. Kind of catching isn't it?

Sparky and Flash just seem to go together naturally and Peewee and Tiny are virtual twins while on the other hand Skinny and Fatty are opposites. For a while I was really fixed on Hammer and Tools but Gunner and Shooter gave me the aim to pick up Sandy and Rocky in my sites and a Cutter being used to Hack a tree that was too Woody. My appetite for the exercise began to improve with Spud and Tater, then I had to go and spoil it all with Poop and Scoop.

I was really on a role with Wheels and Spinner and Boots and Kicker seemed to go together, especially if you're playing soccer. You simply can't have a King without a Queen nor Hands without Fingers. If you're Sleepy you're bound to be a little Dopey and every Digger needs a Spade. Baldy and Curly are at the opposite ends of the follicular spectrum but there's little difference between Smasher and Basher. I couldn't bite into Gummer until I found myself chewing with Toother.

I tried especially hard to keep it all in the family (Rodent, that is) with Mouse and Squirrel and I always kind of felt sorry for Wart and Hog. It is a Bummer when someone shoots the Bull but Grinny and Smiley always put me in a good mood and I would be remiss if I were to Skip old Hoppy.

Beans and Toots gave me just enough gas for a couple more but I had to Stretch to come up with Tippy and Toes, probably because I was about to bog down after Mud and Dirt. So, in conclusion, I pose this nagging question: "Is it true that every Buck is Horny?" After all for every Bang there is a Buck!

As silly as it is, these are all legitimate nicknames to which I can attach proper names and real faces. Now let's get on with more serious thinking—like the state of the economy . . . On second thought, I'd rather stay with nicknames.

P.S.: This item is dedicated to two good friends, Brownie and Blackie.

CHAPTER 24

TURNING GRAINS OF SAND INTO PEARLS

I CANNOT HELP but think that the effective treatment of trouble is splendidlyillustrated by the small oyster, into whose shell one day there comes a tiny grain of sand.

I first became fascinated with oysters when I was given a book on the occasion ofmy birthday about 60 years ago. In "Mr. Jones Meets the Master", prolific Scottish Presbyterian Minister Peter Jones uses the oyster to effectively illustrate the point I want to make. He sets up his story by explaining that by some strange circumstance, a tiny piece of quartz (sand) has entered into the shell of an oyster and there, like an alien thing, an intruder, imposes pain and distress and presents a very real problem.

What is the oyster to do? Well, there are several courses open to it. The oyster could, as so many of us would in a time of adversity and trouble, openly rebel against the sovereign Providence of God. The oyster, metaphorically speaking, could shake a fist and complain bitterly: "Why should this happen to me? Why should I suffer so? What have I done to deserve this? With all the billions of oyster shells up and down the seaboard, why did this grain of sand have to find my shell?"

The oyster could conclude: "There is no justice. Since this calamity has overtaken me, I'll throw away all the faith I ever had. It doesn't do any good anyway."

The oyster could say that, but it doesn't.

Or the oyster could say: "It can't be true. I must not permit myself to believe it." Mustering up its best positive stance in the face of the cruel reality of the painful grain of sand, the oyster could declare that: "There is no such thing as pain. This grain of sand does not make me uncomfortable, and I'm not going to allow my mind to think of it. Instead I will project my thoughts on positive planes of beauty, truth and goodness.

But the oyster does not do that either.

There is another attitude the oyster could adopt, a very commendable one, that calls for a lot of fortitude, courage and determination. The oyster could say: "Now that this hard calamity has overtaken me, this thing that hurts and cuts and stabs, I must endure to the end. I must show everyone that I can take it, and I won't give in, even if it kills me."

But again, the oyster does not do that because it is at one and the same time a realist as well as an idealist. There is no point in trying to deny the reality that tortures every nerve, so the oyster does not try. In spite of all the denial, nothing can change the fact that the grain of sand is there.

The oyster, instead, recognizes the presence of the grim intruder and right away begins to do something. Slowly and patiently, with infinite care, the oyster builds upon the grain of sand—layer upon layer of a plastic, milky substance that covers each sharp corner and coats every cutting edge—and eventually a pearl is made. A thing of wonderous beauty wrapped around trouble.

The remarkable little, seen-one-you've-seen-'em-all oyster has learned to turn grains of sand into pearls that are sought the world over. It has learned to turn cruel misfortunes into blessings and pain and distress into beauty.

Bet you'll never again think the same about oysters—and pearls too, for that matter.

CHAPTER 25

WE REAP WHAT WE SOW IN LIFE

M Y THESIS: LOVE is positive, stronger and always conquers hatred. On the other hand, if you meet hatred with hatred, you simply intensify it.

How earth-shattering and profound can that be? "Not very," you say? But how often we forget! I know that I have had lapses of memory when it came to that age-old truth.

One of the sages that I seem to be in the habit of quoting, has said: "Always meet petulance with gentleness and perverseness with kindness. A gentle hand can lead even an elephant by a hair. Reply to thine enemy with gentleness. Opposition to peace is sin."

How often have we heard the expression, "Never mind, I'll get even with him." But the question remains, will you? And how would you do it? Well, you could do it in one of two ways.

1) You could deal with him as he deals, or apparently deals, with you. Pay him, as we say, in his own coin. In so doing, however, you would get even with the individual by sinking to their level with the result that more often than not the two of you would end up suffering.

Or, 2) you could show yourself to be the larger by demonstrating love in place of hatred, kindness instead of ill-treatment, and in so doing "get even" by raising the other party to the higher level. The upside to this choice of action, of course, is the fact that you can never help another person without actually helping yourself at the same time. Here the old adage: "You reap what you sow!" certainly holds true.

Then there is an often forgotten bonus. The person that we forgive, or help, may just turn around and return the compliment for someone else, thereby contributing to a care-encumbered society. Funny how it works, isn't it?

Suffice to say, we need more gentleness, sympathy and compassion in our common human life today. Just a little something to think about when you have a minute.

CHAPTER 26

THE "WORD" ACCORDING TO ROSANNE

She's in an league by herself

M Y WIFE ROSANNE is a serious female Norm Crosby, the comedic King of Malaprop.

Norm, of course, was famous for the use of twisted phrases in his comedy act. His version of "He had panache", for instance, came out as "He had pistachio." He often talked about drinking "decapitated" coffee. Now compare that to Rosanneisms such as "custody" (custard) tarts and her frequent time "constructions" (constrictions). Certain coffee also leaves a bad "aftermath" (after taste) in her mouth. See what I mean.

A malapropism (from French mal propos) is an incorrect usage of a word, usually with comic effect. The word comes from the name Mrs. Malaprop, a character in Richard Brinsley Sheridan's comedy, The Rivals (1775), whose name was in turn derived from the existing English word malapropos which means "inappropriately". Here are some examples from Mrs. Malaprop's dialogue:

"He's as headstrong as an allegory (alligator) on the banks of the Nile. "He is the very pineapple (pinnacle) of politeness." "If I reprehend (apprehend) anything in this world, it is the use of my oracular (vernacular) tongue, and a nice derangement (arrangement) of epitaphs (epithets)."

Several prominent knowledge bases, however, suggest that it might be more appropriate to call such confusions "Dogberryisms" after Sergeant Dogberry in William Shakespeare's Much Ado About Nothing, who was making them almost two centuries earlier, for example:

"Companions are odorous (odious)."

"Our watch, sir, have indeed comprehended (apprehended) two auspicious (suspicious) persons."

Now back to a few of my favorite malaprops by Rosanne.

The other day she she referred to a situation as being "disconcerning". She meant disconcerting of course. "I can't stand concentration." In this instance she was responding to something that had upset her and it was "consternation" that she was experiencing. On the need to purchase Kleenex. "We've exhorted (exhausted) our supply." "Are you going to have your soul food (seafood) tonight?" quickly recognizing her malapropism by asking me: "What's it called?" "The only player that I know on the Maple Leafs this year is Joseph Curtis." Meaning veteran NHL goaltender Curtis Joseph. Late in the evening of my recent birthday she asked: "Are you going to give me a kiss in the postparten (late stage) of your birthday?" To our dog Lucy who was giving me an affectionate lick on the face: "You certainly know what side your bacon (bread) is buttered on, Lucy." Commenting on a well-known actor who was engaged in a long-standing commonlaw relationship: "He's not going to open the barn door when the cow is free." In this case she gave her twist to several expressions, probably meaning "He's not going to buy the cow when the milk is free." One day she asked me to make a "trilogy" sandwich for lunch. "What's a trilogy sandwich?" I questioned to which she replied: "You know, bacon, cheese, lettuce, tomato, mayo, the works the whole trilogy!" In reference to one of her favorite baseball players: "He's a good sneaker", meaning he is a good base stealer. A self-diagnosis of some stomach discomfort she was experiencing: "I've got a perpendicular problem." I didn't have the heart to ask for further explanation.

Then there was the evening when we had just finished dinner. Rosanne pushed aside her empty plate saying "Why don't we have one of your candy box cookies for dessert?"

"We don't have candy box cookies, but we do have some ice box cookies . . . Would you like one of those?" I asked with a customary smirk. Her response: "Whatever. Have it your way!"

The capper, though, came as a result of my having teased her for some unexplainable reason. "You, you . . ." she gushed, pausing as if searching for something bad enough and sufficiently descriptive . . ."You're nothing but a hyprocondriac(?) gone bad!" Boy, I guess she told me.

That was just a small sample, I could go on endlessly.

Rosanne does not try to be funny with her word twists. She is extremely self expressive, spontaneous and serious about what she says. It's just that the words do not always come out right and even she is at a loss sometimes to explain why. She keeps me in stitches and I tread a fine line in offering corrections because she is priceless and I do not want to make her self-conscious and, in the process, spoil her.

I don't know, but I'll stack Rosanne up against Norm Crosby, Mrs. Malaprop and Sergeant Dogberry any day of the week. Ya gotta love her!

CHAPTER 27

WHAT IS YOUR PASSION?

DICTIONARY DEFINITION FOR the word "passion": An emotion applied to a very strong feeling or desire. Intense, compelling, enthusiastic.

My wife and I were talking the other day about the importance of passion in life. We concluded with the generalization that nothing is achieved without a degree of passion and that working on things that matter to us personally is the key.

When we do things autonomously, purely for the challenge or because of deep passion for a particular undertaking or cause, we can achieve happiness, not only for ourselves but others as well. Passion is all about allowing yourself to get lost in something important to you—a dream, a goal, even a person with whom you have a close attachment.

Passion, I believe, is of utmost importance when we reach midlife. This is a period when we finally have the opportunity to shed the burden of having to live up to the expectations of others—parents, a spouse, children, employers. In mid life we truly need passion that will energize and motivate us and provide us with a guiding force around which to organize the balance of our lives.

Some of us may have carry-over beliefs, concepts and ideas that are keeping us from realizing the passion in our life that we deserve. We need to take a close look at that possibility. A process of elimination may be necessary. Ultimately, identifying our midlife passion(s) will help us make the crucial decisions we all face.

What will we do with our new-found leisure time? What were the day dreams of our youth? What have we always wanted to do but were afraid to try? What are the things that matter most in our lives?

—our children,
—our grandchildren,
—our spouse,
—our work,
—our special interests,
—our religion.

Somewhere in this mix we should be able to identify passions with potential to transcend mere personal pleasure, something that benefits others, makes the world a better place. Something that we can pursue with a whole heart and experience a resultant robustness unknown to our youth.

My old school chum Bob Wilmott and his Ethiopian prison ministry comes immediately to mind as a classic example, although we don't all have to travel across the globe to realize our passion. Bruce Huff is another friend who pursues his over-70s old-timers hockey and slow pitch softball with enthusiasm and a fire in his belly for international competition that is almost unbelievable. Long-time acquaintance Ray Gilbert lives for hunting and fishing and running his beloved ATV machine over the Bruce County terrain and trails that he vigorously promotes. Next door neighbor Art Grady, a former Saskatchewan junior tennis champion, maintains his love for the game and a competitive edge that has lasted well into his late sixties.

Personally, this book and my Wrights Lane web site have become a passion beyond my fondest expectations. I get totally lost in the writing . . . and I do it for my readers too. And something else: I just realized that the above list of potential passions is, in reality, my personal list of passions. I am a lucky guy! My life's cup overflows with passion.

What fuels a fire within you, dear reader? If you can answer that question, then you have identified a bonafide passion. I pray that you will work the daylights out of it—and be lucky like me, Bob Bruce, Ray and Art.

CHAPTER 28

THROUGH THE EYES
OF A CHILD

I AM FASCINATED by children, particularly my grandkids—they seem to inspire me in a number of ways. I have applied that inspiration to much of my writing over the years.

I canot help but discretely study their faces and body language, wishing that I could briefly invade the privacy of their developing minds to find out what they are really thinking and feeling at that particular moment. While you can almost hear the wheels turning, you never seem to be able to get close enough, if you know what I mean, and I find myself reverting to what I may have been thinking and feeling when I was their age.

My attention during a particular weekend visit was drawn to little Madison, then three years of age going on 13. When you have a bubbly three-year-old in your midst you just cannot help but get caught up in their enthusiasm, energy and innocence. I found myself, more than once, thinking how wonderful it would be if we could stay in the mode of a little child all our life—where every valley is green and every rose is red.

Where laughter is always ringing and every smile is real. And where the hurts are little hurts that just a kiss will heal.

Where jealousy, bitterness and strife are unheard of and no one speaks unkindly.

Where peaceful dreams really do come true and the sun is always shining and the sky is for ever blue.

Where each one loves the other and every one is fair; and cheeks are *pink with beauty and singing fills the air.

Where innocence prevails and there is not a thing to dread.

Where care is not an ogre and sin is but a name, and no one thinks of money and no one sighs for fame.

Ah, yes, I yearn for the life of a three-year-old. Heaven can wait!

Meantime, stay as sweet and as innocent as you were then Madi, for as long as you can. Your Poppa will trudge along behind, seeing and feeling life as you do—for as long as he can.

*Madie's favorite color is pink.

DICK WRIGHT

CHAPTER 29

LET A SMILE BE YOUR UMBRELLA

GRANDDAUGHTER MADISON AND MOM CINDY . . .
THAT'S WHAT I'M TALKIN ABOUT!

WE USED TO have a mirror in our bathroom that constantly reminded us to "Smile . . . It increases your face value!" Every time I looked at/in the mirror I had to smile, not just because I enjoy corny puns, but because it simply made me smile. Come on now, you can't even think of the word "smile" without smiling, can you? What are you doing at this very moment, even just a little?

You see, a smile not only increases our own "face value", but it generally increases the face value of the person to whom it is directed. It is truly infectious. Next to a smile, a friendly word or greeting can have a positive impact on another person. I think the two go hand-in-hand. Greet someone with a smile and watch their face light up.

The real significance of the words sprawled across the mirror came into focus one day when I was engaging in a little mind game that I often play called "The trouble with the world is . . ." The silly thought crossed my mind that the world would be a much better place if, somehow, we could provide every home with one of these mirrors. Then I thought "smile pins" or buttons for everyone would be a more practical approach; but even that idea was unrealistic.

Finally, it dawned on me. We don't need staggering sums of money and clever public awareness programs to help make the world smile when every single one of us is capable of tapping into our own love-based thought system. It costs nothing to wear a smile. All we have to do is project ourselves by stepping out of our insular comfort zones more often and to realize that what we see in others is a reflection of our own state of mind. In order for us to change our experience we must first change our thoughts.

Life experience teaches us that only love is real and that to give is to receive. We share love through a smile. We are responsible for the world we see and we choose the feelings that we experience. We alone can decide on the goal we want to achieve. What more, then, do we need to help make the world smile?

Put on a happy face dear friend and have a good life. The world needs an infectous smile like yours!

Thanks for visiting us at Wrights Lane. Next time don't let me monopolize the conversation so much.

DICK WRIGHT